Asperger's Syndrome and Adults…
Is Anyone Listening?

# Asperger's Syndrome and Adults... Is Anyone Listening?

Essays and Poems by Partners, Parents and Family Members of Adults with Asperger's Syndrome

*Collected by Karen E. Rodman*

Families of Adults Afflicted with Asperger's Syndrome
FAAAS Inc.

*Foreword by Dr Tony Attwood*

Jessica Kingsley Publishers
London and Philadelphia

First published in the United Kingdom in 2003
by Jessica Kingsley Publishers
116 Pentonville Road
London N1 9JB, UK
and
400 Market Street, Suite 400
Philadelphia, PA 19106, USA

*www.jkp.com*

Copyright © Jessica Kingsley Publishers 2003
Printed digitally since 2010

**Library of Congress Cataloging in Publication Data**
A CIP catalog record for this book is available from the Library of Congress

**British Library Cataloguing in Publication Data**
A CIP catalogue record for this book is available from the British Library

ISBN 978 1 84310 751 4

# Contents

*For all of the spouses and
partners and families whose lives
were filled with loneliness,
sadness, frustration and chaos and
then they found the medical term:
Asperger's Syndrome.*

*Within these pages
may you find validation.*

# Acknowledgements

We want to thank profoundly those who were willing to describe their confused and broken hearts, their unfulfilled dreams... because of what was, until quite recently, an unrecognized medical disorder. May this book be just the beginning!

Our heart-felt thanks to Susan Low-Beer for allowing us to reprint a photo-image of one of her pieces of sculpture as the logo for FAAAS Inc.

Our thanks to Drs Edward and Riva Ritvo and Dr Linda Demer, of UCLA, for their staunch support and input.

If we began acknowledging everyone who has made an effort on our behalf, we would have to have another book just for their names! Suffice it to say that we are beholden to one and all...you have our undying gratitude.

This page would not be complete if the name of Tony Attwood, PhD was not mentioned. Without Tony Attwood's support, our concerns and issues would have taken much longer to be recognized and validated. Thank you, Tony, from the families of adults afflicted with Asperger's Syndrome, from around the world.

Ruth and Frank Norton, dear friends who have emotionally supported me and FAAAS Inc. since the very beginning of this venture.

Anne Henry, my dear friend, who has assisted me in numerous ways. The past few months would never have happened without her support and help.

# Terminology

Autism Spectrum Disorder (ASD), also called Pervasive
  Developmental Disorder (PDD):
    Describes a range of behaviors generally related to
    impaired social interaction or communication, and
    repetitive patterns of behavior, interest and activities,
    from mild to severe. Includes autism, Asperger's
    Syndrome, and Pervasive Developmental Disorder
    Not Otherwise Specified.

Asperger's Syndrome (AS):
    A neurological/biological/medical disorder on the
    autistic spectrum. Also referred to as higher
    functioning autism.

Aspie:    How some with AS refer to themselves.

Cassandra Phenomenon:
    The state of mind and stress which affects members
    of families where autistic spectrum disorders are
    present.

Neurotypicals (NT):
    People who are not afflicted with Asperger's
    Syndrome.

Pervasive Developmental Disorder Not Otherwise Specified
  (PDD-NOS):
    A diagnosis of pervasive impairment in the
    development of reciprocal social interaction or verbal
    and nonverbal communication skills, or when
    stereotyped behavior, interests and activities are
    present, but the criteria are not met for other
    diagnoses.

# Foreword

If you are reading this foreword, then you are one of the first to listen to the voices of those who have a partner, parent or family member with Asperger's Syndrome. There are several "pathways" to opening and reading this book. The most likely "pathway" is being someone who has a child who has been diagnosed as having Asperger's Syndrome. Discovery of the range of expression of the syndrome, especially in adults, can lead to the realization that the child's father or mother also has the same profile of abilities, although to a less conspicuous degree; the child may not be the only person in the family with signs of Asperger's Syndrome.

Another pathway is to recognize the characteristics in one of your parents. The characteristics may have "skipped" a generation and this book will help explain the difficulties experienced by a typical child in his or her attempts at forming a relationship with a parent with Asperger's Syndrome. Having a father or mother with Asperger's Syndrome may also partially explain the type of person who becomes your partner.

The third pathway is being a person with Asperger's Syndrome who may have or anticipates having a partner, or being the parents of an adolescent preparing for the long-term future of their son or daughter. Recognizing the potential problems in a relationship where one partner has Asperger's Syndrome can be an opportunity to avoid a dysfunctional relationship and instead encourage a successful partnership and family. Prevention of relationship problems is better than having to rely on relationship therapy.

The fourth pathway is being a specialist in Asperger's Syndrome or a relationship counselor. We are only just discovering the upper end of the continuum of expression of Asperger's Syndrome and how to understand and help such individuals and their families. Adults with Asperger's Syndrome can have intimate relationships but the nature of Asperger's Syndrome can have a significant effect on the partnership and on the psychological development of children. When a relationship develops, there can be problems with communication, affection, empathy, expectations and emotions that can benefit from relationship counseling. However, relationship counselors may have little training, knowledge or experience in helping a partnership where one person has Asperger's Syndrome.

The effects of having a parent or partner with Asperger's Syndrome can also lead to the development of signs of chronic stress, depression, and subsequent medical and psychological disorders. That person may need medical and psychological treatment by a specialist who listens to and understands both parties in the relationship. The second part of the title of the book, *Is Anyone Listening?*, is very appropriate. When no one is listening, there are inevitable feelings of not being believed, being blamed, and disappointment in professional support. This book is a guide for partners, families and professionals.

Karen Rodman has collected essays and poems from around the world that illustrate and help to explain the perspective and experiences of both partners and how Asperger's Syndrome can affect the whole family. Her compassion and insight are quite remarkable and have been a beacon of light for those in the dark depths of despair. The book alerts and validates. Both partners will recognize that their credibility and sanity are not on trial, and will empathize with the descriptions of events, thoughts and reactions. There are also indicators of what to do to rescue the relationship or to plan for a different future.

*Dr Tony Attwood*

# Preface

If we all speak up, tell our separate stories, "open up the windows" on the truth of the behaviors of adults with Asperger's Syndrome, and how these AS behaviors, until now unrecognized by the professionals, affect the entire family, the journey for the children with AS will be much easier in the future.

We can help prevent another generation of families from living through the pain and frustration and torment of not knowing about this disorder – in infants, children, and in adults – by being forthcoming...telling our stories.

The professionals can help by listening to us, and validating our lives, thereby educating themselves about the behaviors of adults with AS from the experts...the families, the people who live with the disorder 24/7.

The earlier in life children are diagnosed correctly, and with the proper training, services, etc., the better it will be for them, their families, and ultimately for society.

*Karen E. Rodman, USA, 2002*

# 1

# Asperger's Syndrome and its Effects Upon the Families

You would probably not be reading this book if you were not aware of Asperger's Syndrome aka AS – specifically AS in adults, and how the behaviors of this disorder affect the entire family unit.

People from around the world are visiting FAAAS Inc.'s website and/or contacting FAAAS, requesting information, the names of clinicians who can evaluate and treat an adult in their family in their area, reassurances that *they* are not crazy, and asking if there is a FAAAS Inc. chapter in their town or city. The majority of people who contact FAAAS are relieved to find a website with information about the effects of AS upon the families, where they can "recognise" how the behaviors of AS affects them, for the first time. Numerous adults who have lived a lifetime on the "outside" looking in, read our website and recognize themselves as an adult who has lived with AS and had never been diagnosed, treated, or been recognized as having a neurological/medical disorder, because they were told they were crazy, or were just "misfits."

The only means of supporting and validating these families that we have right now is our website, our international listserve, *The Book of FAAAS*, our international conferences, and the support and recognition of *our* aspect of AS from Tony Attwood, PhD, and a few others who also have the knowledge of the behaviors of adults who are on the autistic spectrum and how these behaviors can raise havoc not only within the life of the person who has AS, but also within the family unit, and at the workplace.

Our objective is to bring the families' knowledge of AS behaviors to the medical communities, the educational communities, the religious and the judicial communities. Adults with AS are suffering, along with their families, because this disorder has not been recognized, has not been diagnosed correctly, has not been treated appropriately, and they have not been given the support and assistance they desperately need. Our aim is to at least bring the term AS into the public arena where it belongs. We hope to help to inform the public that autism/AS is *not* a mental disorder, but it is a neurological/medical problem that needs to be recognized in early infancy. If early diagnosis and the correct intervention is made available, these children's lives will be made much easier, assimilating into society throughout their childhood, their adolescent years, and into adulthood. We do not want to see another generation of AS lives ruined because of lack of knowledge of undiagnosed, unrecognized, incorrectly treated adults who have AS. And it is not only the person who has unrecognized AS whose life is in shambles...AS affects the spouses/partners, the children they bring into this world, the parents, the siblings.

The fall-out of the effects of AS behaviors continues *ad infinitum* if the disorder is left untreated, unrecognized.

*FAAAS Inc., USA, 2002*

*2*

# Cassandra Phenomenon

Many of the people who attend FAAAS conferences are spouses/partners, parents, siblings, or NT children of an ASD parent. The information we can give to the medical communities is unfathomable…but few in the medical communities are willing to *listen* to us. For years we were considered "crabby", highly emotional, overly sensitive, sickly, moody. Doctors *never* asked or cared what our private lives were like…and when they did ask we were told to: "pull it together", "Life is not a 'rose garden,' don't be so picky, what *is* your problem?!" They did not realize or recognize the fact that we were suffering from post-traumatic stress disorder or, as we refer to it, the "Cassandra Phenomenon".

The "Cassandra Phenomenon" was given its name from a character in Greek mythology, in Homer's *Odyssey*.

Cassandra, one of Priam's daughters, was a prophetess. The god Apollo fell in love with her and, as a token of his love, gave her the power to foretell the future. Later, he became bitter because she refused his love. Although he could not take back the gift of prophecy once it was bestowed, he added a curse that no one would believe her prophecies.

It was her fate always to know the disasters that were coming and yet be unable to avert them. When she declared that the Greeks were hidden in the wooden horse given as a present to the Trojans, no one gave her words a thought. After she was taken captive years later, the people heard of her strange fame as a prophetess whom no one ever believed and yet whose prophecies were always true.

This is the parallel to our stories, our lives. No one believed us either until now. The "Cassandra Phenomenon" is now our name for the "disorder" which affects members of families where autistic spectrum disorders are present. We were not believed or listened to by professionals, medical, spiritual, educational, or judicial leaders. We have had to forge ahead on our own, struggling, step by step, without any assistance, support or backing.

Now we have the seeds of groups around the world, all with the same mission...to tell the public, the medical, the educational, and the judicial communities that Asperger's Syndrome, a neurological/biological/medical disorder on the autistic spectrum, *exists*, and that we are the living proof of its possible fall-out. We are "the invisible walking wounded".

*We* are Cassandra.

*FAAAS Inc., USA, 2000*

*3*

# The Family Aspect of Asperger's Syndrome

Parents of autistic children suffered a tragic injustice only a few decades ago that is being relived by families of adults with undiagnosed Asperger's Syndrome. Dr Bruno Bettelheim and his followers in the psychoanalytical field blamed autism on parents, especially mothers, whom he labeled "refrigerator mothers." This authoritative erroneous doctrine kept autism research in the dark ages, to the detriment of many. Thanks to the courage of a small number of parents, vindication has come, though too late for some. In retrospect, it seems so clear that telling parents they caused the autism by "subconscious rejection" only added overwhelming pain, guilt and frustration to the already challenging lives of those who lovingly cared for their autistic children. In many cases, this resulted in institutionalization of the child. This injustice was the topic of a recent documentary, and it is widely appreciated that we should not let such a disaster recur. Today there are abundant supports for parents of children with autism spectrum disorders, including AS national organizations, seminars, research foundations, articles, conferences, public sympathy and support groups for and about children with these disorders.

Nevertheless, history cycles. The first sign is the conspicuous lack of acknowledgement that children with AS actually grow up to become adults with AS. A hush surrounds the concept. Some have the impression that either the disorder, or the individuals who have it, vanish by age 18. Instead, these largely undiagnosed adults are involved in public and private human interactions that can be destructive in the absence of awareness and support. The tragedy is unintentional psychological and emotional brutality. It is a culprit-less crime. Nothing more than the diagnostic features of AS are needed to appreciate the potential harm to others. These include rigidity, lack of compassion, egocentricity, lack of empathy, misinterpretation of intentions, difficulty anticipating or appreciating others' feelings, lack of remorse, emotional inaccessibility, and inability to establish relationships. Life with an uncompensated, undiagnosed adult is almost necessarily painful and frustrating. The impact on his or her children may be profound but is not yet known.

Unfortunately, when relatives of adults with AS seek help in the USA, they often confront the same prejudice as did parents of children with autism. Many counselors are not aware that AS persists to adulthood or that individuals with autism spectrum disorders do marry and have children. The frightened or distraught relatives are often blamed for the problems and labeled as emotionally needy. This natural response adds familiar pain, guilt and frustration to the lives of those who have been lovingly caring for their relative. In many cases, this results in breakdown of the relationship, separation, or divorce. Fortunately, experts in England are aware of such issues, and they have established programs to be sure the disorder is recognized and that the relatives receive support and understanding to continue their effort to support their loved one.

A cute story is floated around support groups for parents of children with autism. Finding out your child has autism is said to be analogous to finding out your long-anticipated trip to Italy has been detoured to Holland. The idea is that Holland is simply a different kind of trip, and that if you spend the time despairing that it is not Italy, you will miss the joys of the windmills and tulips. To many, this is a valuable paradigm. The important difference for the family of the undiagnosed adult with AS can be illustrated as a modified parable. Imagine your trip to Italy is detoured to Holland, but everyone there, including your relative with AS, the tour guides, and the tour books all insist that it IS Italy. Your efforts to convince them it's Holland are so confidently and authoritatively denied that you begin to doubt your own sanity.

*Linda Demer, MD, PhD,*
*Guthman Professor of Medicine and Physiology*
*at the David Geffen School of Medicine at UCLA, 2002*

*4*

# Things I Have Learnt About Asperger's Syndrome After Seven Years' Campaigning for Support for Families

One thing I have learnt about people with Asperger's Syndrome (AS) is that you cannot say "they" do this or "they" do that; it depends on where they are on the spectrum and how many "blind spots" they have in each area of social interaction, communication, imagination, sensory sensitivity and clumsiness. Very slight impairments can be extremely subtle to detect but still cause havoc for the person and his or her family or work colleagues. Human relationships are built on communication, so trying to relate to a person with AS has inbuilt difficulties. Many have a high IQ, which adds to the mystery of why an intelligent person does such apparently stupid things, or why a basically kind person can do such unkind things and be so lacking in consideration or awareness.

The stereotype of an odd, isolated loner with no friends, eye contact or emotional involvement is not accurate for all. Many have friends, good eye contact and are affectionate and emotionally involved; their impairments are in different areas but still involve social boundaries. Some are very sociable, may dive in where they are not wanted and can appear to do things which are audacious, or cheeky, to "have a nerve". Each is differently and uniquely affected. (One lady invites herself to be included in the plans of others with no idea that she may not be wanted or checking if it is convenient. One lady always goes to the front of a queue. One lady went to a wedding reception and the bar in the lounge was not open. She went behind the bar and started serving drinks. One young man, when eating with friends, would help himself to a "taste" from their plate without asking, and because he said they could do the same did not see that this was anti-social.)

What you can say about all people with AS is that they will sometimes exhibit "behavior which is not appropriate to the situation". Anti-social behavior which they do not know is considered anti-social; they do not know what being anti-social is. Astonishment that anyone should be upset or offended by what they have said or done. (Cracking jokes at funerals because everyone is too solemn, smiling while telling you that a family member is in hospital. Falling asleep at work. Not telling you when something has happened which will have an impact on you, but expecting you to know. One man had a caravan at the seaside and invited his brother and future sister-in-law to use it for their honeymoon. The week before the wedding the bride asked what the arrangements were to get the key to the caravan, and he said, "Oh, I've sold it!")

Behavior that reminds you of Jekyll and Hyde can be charming or vitriolic. Can appear "normal" at work but the stress this creates is all vented at home. Often it is the wife or mother who bears the brunt of Mr Hyde. Attempts at behavior modification can mean going from one extreme to the other. (One wife said her husband never paid her compliments, and he complimented her twenty-five times during the next twenty-four hours, even when she didn't look nice. He was then offended because she said it didn't seem sincere and he was doing what she had said. When the work of an employee was criticized, one man said, "OK, I'll sack her.") Anxiety can be out of all proportion to what caused it.

They find our behavior as baffling as we find theirs. Why don't we mean what we say and say what we mean? We use a lot of metaphorical speech, which they may take literally. (One young lady who went to see a psychiatrist was asked, "Do you hear voices?" She replied, "Yes," was diagnosed schizophrenic and treated accordingly. Years later she was correctly diagnosed as having AS. She replied "Yes" because you do not see voices or smell voices or taste voices, you hear voices. She missed the real meaning of the question: "Do you hear voices when there is nobody there?" Or: "Do you imagine you hear voices?" A young boy sitting in a psychologist's room was asked to take his book out; he went outside in the corridor. A child asked to "go and ask mummy if she wants a cup of tea" doesn't realize you want the child to come back and tell you what she said.)

Metaphors are part of our language and communication; people pick up on the allusion, it resonates meaning, makes sense of ideas or concepts. (Toast the bride, run like clockwork, run on ahead, pulling your leg, frog in the throat, down in the mouth, ship-shape. One man who was called a bluebeard because he was two-timing his wife thought they meant he needed a shave.) Being polite, strongly indicating, hints and tact are often useless; wishes must be spelt out in a very clear, direct manner.

AS is about missing the meaning, missing the point, misunderstanding and misinterpretation of intention. Missing links in the circuits in the social brain. It is about being accused of not listening, being able to repeat word for word exactly what was said, but not comprehending the meaning of what was said. It is about missing the meaning in facial expression, tone of voice, or body language. Not understanding sarcasm. A person may think someone is romantically interested in him or her when just being kind or friendly. (One young man's girlfriend of several months went to bed with him and nothing happened because he didn't know if she wanted him to. One young man met a girl on a week's holiday and pestered his social worker to facilitate his move to the hostel in the town where she lived. In spite of his family's foreboding this was done. Nobody realized that he had not informed the young lady of his intentions. She became anxious and felt threatened and her family removed her. He couldn't understand where he had "gone wrong" and became depressed.)

People with AS often don't recognize the emotional needs of others or understand that they have emotional needs; they may not recognize their own feelings or understand what they are, even feeling hungry or full. They can't see things from another's point of view, put themselves in their shoes. They may get angry because they think someone is "having a go" at them when all they are doing is explaining or querying. They may think you are angry when you are upset or sad. They may accuse you of awful things because they have misunderstood, and cannot comprehend that you just would not do such a thing, or that there are hidden intentions or joint intentions. They may appear not to know your character even after a lifetime of living together. (One man seeing people exchanging glances or "knowing looks" asked what they were doing with their eyes.) They are often not able to generalize social rules learnt to cover a specific situation, and vice versa.

People with AS may be vulnerable to exploitation, may not see malicious intent. (One young man who had worked in a jeweller's for several months handed over a tray of rings to a caretaker who had "befriended" him.) They may get in trouble with the law because of lack of understanding of social rules, social conformity etc., or may know the law but ignore it if it interferes with their plans. (One young man stole a train. They were his obsession and he knew all about them; he just got in at the station and drove off. One man who parked illegally returned to his car to find a policewoman there. He said he could not stop because he was late for work. He got in his car so she opened the passenger door and got in the car. He drove off to work and was arrested for kidnap, among other things.)

They may be on the receiving end of anger and hostility because of behavior which upsets or offends. They are very vulnerable to depression and suicide, especially if there is a growing awareness of their difference which they do not understand or know how to deal with, or they do not understand why things keep going wrong for them. They may use alcohol or drugs as an escape. They may be very bad with money, not understand how credit cards work, be bad at organizing time, coping with criticism. They may refuse to do something at work because they do not want to do it, don't understand social or moral obligation, that a promise is a binding verbal contract.

They do not get the understanding and support needed because nobody knows they have a problem, and others think they are just awful people. (One young man went for a driving test. The windows steamed up and the examiner pointed this out but the man just carried on. At the end of the test the examiner said to the instructor, "Does he come from a mental home?" The young man was very upset and when his mother asked why he didn't clear the windows when the examiner pointed this out, he said, "But he didn't tell me to".)

It is a double-edged tragedy for the person with AS and for the non-autistic person who tries to have a normal relationship with him or her; many say it is like living with an alien. They can appear to be indifferent, aloof, detached, unemotional (not greeting visitors who have just driven 300 miles to see them), callous, not show concern when you are ill or if there is a bereavement, not notice when you are in trouble and need help. (One wife sat on a beach chair which gave way and she fell through the seat, wedged and unable to move. Her husband sitting opposite just looked at her. Another husband didn't visit his wife in the hospital when she was having a baby. One woman had to ask a friend to take her and the baby home. The husband of a very sick wife asked would she get him his dinner. In the case of another sick wife, the husband fed himself but not the children. A father didn't visit his daughter in hospital for five days because he said there was nothing he could do.)

People with AS can have impaired parenting skills, not understanding childhood developmental stages, and may not notice their child with AS has problems and needs help. They may not be able to give help suggested because they do not understand what the matter is. They can show a lack of awareness of potentially dangerous situations (particularly involving electricity) or knowing how to act in them. (For example, not getting a child to hospital after an accident. One father put a three-year-old out in the front garden to play; the garden was open plan with no fence to the road. Another father put a two-year-old in bath water which was too hot. A mother made sandwiches with mouldy bread and put damp sheets on the bed. A father boarded up the front and back doors while his wife was out for lunch because he had not wanted her to go, and there were two infants in the house. Another shaved the head of a neighbour's child he was babysitting.) There can be emotional, mental and psychological abuse of partners and children, even sometimes physical or sexual.

Because in the past it was mostly boys who were taken to the doctor by parents anxious about their development, researchers believed that of people affected by autism three out of four were male. This is not borne out by evidence from families; many have identified a mother or mother-in-law, sister or daughter with Asperger traits which they only recognized when reading literature after a child was diagnosed. Dr Tony Attwood says that because girls have naturally higher verbal and social skills, their symptoms are different and they can be missed, and this appears to be what is actually happening. It is also very difficult to find men with an Asperger wife who are prepared to talk about it.

People with AS are in all walks of life. It is now thought to affect 3 in 100 primary school children and, as autistic spectrum disorders are strongly hereditary, for every child diagnosed there are likely to be other family members affected. Dr Tony Attwood says universities are sheltered workshops for people with AS. Symptoms can be lack of common sense, underdeveloped conscience, lack of remorse, not able to see cause and effect or consequences, and impaired people management skills. Impaired perception means impaired judgement because a situation has not been accurately read. And there are people with AS who are judges, solicitors, doctors, politicians, civil servants, policemen, town planners, teachers, nurses, social workers, businessmen, military officers, etc.

People with AS go on jury duty. People in positions of power and authority may make decisions which are short-sighted, short term, they may be unable to think them through and see the consequences, which may have a very bad effect on other people. Administration is often confused because of an inability to see the whole picture, just focusing on details. People with AS who have to do performance management assessments of subordinates may be very unfair and unjust. They may sabotage others' plans and can be malicious, prejudiced, resist change and may be drawn to organizations which have fanatical religious or political views.

People who have realized that their partners have Asperger's Syndrome are placed in an unenviable position. Relief is enormous with the realization that there is a reason for the partners' behavior; they were not deliberately hurting them, they were born with this condition and it was not their fault. There is a feeling of exoneration that they were right, there was something the matter, it was not their fault, and anger at all the therapists, counselors, etc. consulted over the years, uneducated in Asperger's, who had dumped the blame for the marriage difficulties squarely on their shoulders.

Then there may be a grieving time similar to bereavement when it is realized that there is no cure for Asperger's; there is never going to be the true partnership or relationship they have worked so hard to achieve. There may be a realization that children are suffering from a lack of parenting skills. Some think that now they know what the matter is they will be able to work at understanding how their partner is affected and try to avoid the triggers for the AS behavior. Some think that their partner will accept the diagnosis and want to work at modifying his or her behavior to improve the relationship and maybe save the marriage, and it can be devastating if they find he or she still cannot see any reason why his or her behavior should be upsetting and therefore will not try to change it.

Many partners have to face the question, "Should I go or should I stay?" Many feel they have to try every therapy/diet/approach that anybody else has found helpful, give it one more chance, one last shot, go the extra mile one more time. Some find that they are able to accept the circumstances of their own particular situation, because there is more positive than negative, the good outweighs the bad. Some feel they cannot go because their partner could not manage without them, or they would not be able to manage financially. Then they may find that trying to build a life of their own, with their own friends, interests and separate finances, will ensure their survival within the marriage.

Some Asperger people can be motivated to try to change if they feel it is for their benefit. If an Asperger trained counselor can be found, this may be invaluable in helping to sort things out. Unfortunately they are very few and far between and most partners don't talk about the very damaging side of Asperger behavior to family and friends because it makes them feel disloyal. Because it is not intentional they do not look on it as abuse. The FAAAS mailing list is where many partners find the validation and comfort to start their healing process, and the strength to face the decisions which must be made.

If, after trying everything, a partner feels there is no alternative but to separate, careful plans must be made for housing, jobs, finances, child care, etc., preferably while you can still think in a calm, reasonable, unemotional state and before you say anything about it. Separating finances should be one of the first things done so you have control of your own money. Some Asperger partners may react in a very unpredictable way to the idea of separation or divorce, feel they are losing control, be very difficult, uncooperative, make unreasonable demands, start divorce proceedings themselves, demand custody of the children even though they are unable to look after them, refuse to leave the house, demand that you leave the house, lie or give inaccurate information about finances, etc. If you can find a solicitor educated in Asperger's who is not affected personally, so much the better, and it may be a good idea to have an emergency plan, just in case it is needed.

*Brenda Wall, UK, 2002*

*5*

# Behind a Glass Wall

I long to reach you
so I stretch out my hand
but I touch a thick glass wall
and I don't understand.

I think that it's me
something that I've done
so I try double time,
to reach you precious one.

But your feelings are locked away
behind that thick glass wall
and you don't care or even hear
my heartache and desperate call.

I haven't always understood
that you can't connect with me.
I thought you cruelly rejected
my deepest self you see.

My deepest self that *feels*
and expresses not in words
an inflexion or a tone of voice
or body language that occurs.

My precious lonely husband
behind glass you're locked away.
My eyes can see a smorgasbord
but I'm starving every day.

93% of communication
is not spoken literal words
body language and tone of voice,
is not just for the birds.

I feel like I'm starving
in the midst of a feast.
I feel abandoned and abused
to say the very least.

I've tried to break the glass
to reach you precious one.
But the more desperate that I get
the more abusive you become.

I've raged in anger and disbelief
that you couldn't open the door.
'Til I finally realized the glass is sealed
and it's pointless to try any more.

In the meantime I must learn
to turn the other cheek
through mockery and sarcastic words
when revenge is what I seek.

And I must grow in love and patience
and forgiveness and long-suffering too
through the long and empty hours
of the silent unreachable you.

When I feel like I don't exist
with loneliness way beyond bearing
and anger rises to irrational heights
at this lack of nurture and caring.

With Asperger's Syndrome
there are the valleys of silence,
until frustration leads you
to the mountains of violence.

Silence begins to climb the mountain
with arguments and debating
leading to abuse and door-slamming
then retreats to the silence abating.

The cycle is very predictable
because you're trapped in that glass wall
and silence or violence is the only way
you can express your FEELINGS at all.

On a factual logical level
your mind is very clear.
And business associates would never guess
that your FEELINGS are trapped in fear.

*6*

# Is Anyone Listening?

We, the families with our blistered hearts and souls and damaged psyche, are the end-product of undiagnosed and untreated Asperger's Syndrome. How many of us are out there? Far too many, I am afraid.

The feelings of rejection and loneliness play a major role in the lives of the Asperger family. You and your feelings are not recognized or understood by the afflicted person. You keep giving and giving and trying to change your behavior and ideas and ideals, your hopes and dreams, to "make peace." You try to please someone who doesn't need or want your emotions, your thoughts or your feelings. He or she does not comprehend what you are trying so desperately to convey. Daily living is like a prison with no boundaries.

His or her inability to respond to you emotionally robs you of your self-esteem, friends, family, confidence in yourself and your confidence in others. It steals a "normal life" away from "normal" people. Those born with the affliction of Asperger's Syndrome survive at the emotional and psychological expense of others. Of course, this is not done consciously on their part!

This is the agony of Asperger's Syndrome. Those afflicted cannot relate to our pain.

The pain is in us, the spouses, the parents and the siblings, not the person with the diagnosis of Asperger's Syndrome. Yes, we should help them! We should do everything humanly possible to make it easier for them to live in our world. But at whose expense? What about those of us who have had to live in their world for years?

Where do we go? What should we do, the spouses, the parents, the siblings? We are the bearers of this emotional pain in this unrelenting abnormality. Where do we, the "walking wounded," go for help?

*Karen E. Rodman, USA, 1997*
*© FAAAS Inc., 2000*

*7*

# Be Careful What You Wish For

I don't know why I've stayed with my AS husband all these years. We've been together 25 years, married 21 years. I've always had the feeling that he can't help being the way he is. When I discovered Asperger's Syndrome a few months ago, suddenly everything made sense. I compiled a list of my husband's "eccentricities," which was incredibly helpful because I was able to look objectively at his symptoms, and see clearly that I've been dealing with an unusual marriage partner. I've had more than one therapist advise me to leave him, because he can be quite emotionally abusive. Our three teenagers are wonderful kids, and I want to stay in the marriage. Sometimes I don't know if I can. I know that I have an amazing ability to "bounce back." He was very smart to choose a partner who is very adaptable, and who also loves to nurture. Well, if I needed someone to nurture, I sure did get what I wished for!

Here's a short description of my husband's Asperger traits. He's never been officially diagnosed, but we both feel he meets the diagnostic criteria. We haven't seen any reason to get him officially diagnosed.

My husband can't whisper, he speaks loudly all of the time, he can't understand facial expressions, he can't "read" mood cues, he'll bump into every single person he passes in a crowded room and not realize it, he can "play back" a movie, scene by scene. He's unable to make the "leaps" in conversations – the kind of leaps most people can make, such as when it is obvious that the speaker is talking about, say, the hairdresser and not the woman getting her hair cut. If you interrupt him mid-sentence, he has to start the sentence over again from the beginning. He's unable to keep our house neat, but his obsessions, such as his comic-book collection, and his movie collection are eerily tidy. When we go to school functions (we have three children), I've grown accustomed to saying things like "There's Donna, Kyle's mom, we're friendly with her." This is because he can't recognize most people, especially people who aren't important to him. And yet he *can* recognize movie stars, isn't that strange?

Anyway, most of our problems revolve around the assumption that *I'm* an extension of him, and that I want to please him all of the time. But when I don't, or when I can't please him, all hell breaks loose. A few times I threatened to leave him, but of course that would mean he has nobody to "hold him together" and so he frantically convinces me to stay. We've had fights that make me feel crazy, for he switches argument tactics so rapidly it's dizzying. Our fights, over the years, have gotten quite physical, and quite scary. Later, he thinks it was all no big deal; as a matter of fact, he literally forgets the fights ever happened.

Our fights have completely ceased, thanks to our self-diagnosis of Asperger's Syndrome. Now they no longer make any sense, at least not to me. I have accepted some new information. He is never going to change. He is never going to mellow out. He is never going to feel empathetic toward me. I'm in a stage of sadness, wondering how I feel about this new version of my husband. I'm relieved to be finished with the big fights. And yet fights involve a kind of optimism that the other person will change. I miss that optimism. I miss feeling hopeful.

My husband has found a job where his eccentricities are accepted and even considered fascinating. I wish many things, mostly that I'd found out about Asperger's Syndrome 25 years ago.

*Anonymous, New Jersey, 2002*

# 8

# Asperger's Dungeon

Like an object,
I was chosen by you.
Like a leech you clung,
I hadn't a clue.

I was part of a plan,
Of which you construed.
Disguised was a future,
Which only you knew.

From deception you hid,
So skillfully, through and through.
A master of disguise,
Coping mechanisms too.

Once in your dungeon,
You throw away the key.
Off comes the mask,
The charade is achieved.

I can not comprehend just what it is I see.
I look up perplexed,
Humiliated and embarrassed,
For the path was hidden well,
Through a lifetime of habit.

Naked on the dungeon floor,
I lie cold with little light.
The chains are woven around me,
Your hold is mighty tight.

Time withers by slowly,
As I feel my soul decay.
I struggle to break free,
I just can't find the way.

Your intentions weren't as cold,
As they may have first appeared.
I just can't understand,
Why you brought me here?

The solution isn't clear,
As I sadly slip away.
For Asperger's claimed another victim,
In its dungeon is where I lay.

*Dawn O'Neil, USA, 2002*

9

# Living With an AS Son

Starting at sixteen, our difficult son was diagnosed and treated by different psychiatrists: first as bipolar, then bipolar with psychotic aspects, then bipolar and ADD, then only bipolar, only ADD – what a nightmare of trial and error with medications, not to mention self-medication, C tried.

Finally last fall, a psychiatrist in Dallas, while I was talking to her about C, said, "This sounds like Asperger's Syndrome to me." This is the first psychiatrist who put all of his early history and medical evaluations together and said, "Asperger." C is now twenty-four. In retrospect, every psychiatrist said, "He has autistic tendencies," and "This is a most difficult case." Which meant not full-blown anything that they understood. So I ordered Tony Attwood's books and started reading.

I'm not sure at all about the bipolar diagnosis (mixed states rapid cycling which sounds like a big "who knows"). In many ways, we can see Asperger and we can see ADD. Much of it fits but not all. If you combined AS and extreme ADD, you would have C. The most important part so far is that he is taking responsibility for his care for the first time. He is now seeing this psychiatrist by his request (he hates psychiatrists but seems to trust her), keeping appointments, and working with her on medication.

C recently met another person with "autism" and said, "I'm just like him. We even talk alike!" He was excited about it. We talked about AS briefly. I showed him the books. Later he read a page from Attwood's workbook for AS adults and said, "*That's me.*"

My husband and I just want to find ways to cope with him. We have spent twenty-four years keeping him alive, creating prosthetic environments, and protecting him from the world that never seems to fit him. He is in his own apartment (that we pay for) because living with him in the house was more than we could stand. We all walk on "egg shells" to keep him happy when he is around because "If C ain't happy, ain't nobody happy!"

When C was three, he said, "Mommy, I love you so much. I want to live with you forever." My husband's response was, "I consider that a threat!" And C wants to live with us because he is lonely. My husband says that it would be the end of his sanity and there is no way. I'm caught in the middle but know my husband is right. C thinks everyone in the family is very nervous, uptight, and unhappy. When he is around, we are! He has no idea how happy, serene and relaxing our lives are when he is not around.

From the age of two, we knew C was the most self-centered child we had ever encountered. (I'm a teacher and counselor and I've seen a lot of kids.) This has not changed. In the light of AS, it makes sense. One psychiatrist diagnosed "Narcissistic personality disorder" when he was sixteen but he had been that way since the beginning. This was not a gradual disintegration.

He was extremely verbal, very high IQ. He is also athletic. "Clumsiness" is only evident in the shape of his clothes and the condition of his carpet. Spots everywhere. When we moved him into his own apartment, the first thing we did was have our carpets cleaned!

He is incapable of seeing another person's point of view. His personality is more like a pit bull terrier. To make him let go of an idea, even a bad one, you would have to beat him to death. We have always referred to this as the "locked-in" behavior of ADD but it is more than that. He sees only one version of everything – his. He honestly can't imagine why someone would have a different opinion when he is obviously right. He doesn't believe you are listening to him unless you agree with him. His idea of a discussion is to get louder than you and, if that doesn't convince you, try using obscene words as adjectives.

When he misunderstands something that we say, he will later insist that we are lying and that we can't remember anything because of our age (fifty-two and fifty-six!). It is hard to interact with him when he is like this, and of course he is always like this.

When he was little, he had one friend at a time and they had to do what he wanted. He was very creative and funny and always had a friend willing to let him lead. When he and a friend wrestled, C could never understand "stop." They had to hurt him to make him stop and then he was surprised.

As a child, he never understood that we were unhappy with him until we were angry. Nothing short of raising our voice and being angry seemed to reach him. On the other hand, he could be very affectionate and loving and seemed to need holding all the time. That's still pretty much the case.

At eighteen, his nineteen-year-old girlfriend whom he had known for a short time got pregnant. She was overwhelmed with his sudden and complete devotion and needed someone to love her. Love may be blind, but she had discovered what living with C was like by the time our grandson was born. They made two years together before she couldn't stand any more. His rages were unreasonable and unpredictable. He couldn't imagine why she needed to sleep when he didn't. He had no idea why she was tired just because she was taking care of a baby. None of his decisions made sense.

He wanted to go to college but he didn't want to go to class. He would drink beer, stay up all night, sleep through classes, and then complain because he had to work part-time. He has gone through countless semester starts without completion, more jobs than you can imagine with long periods of unemployment. When the stress builds up, he shuts down. From June of last year to February of this year, he was not working. Now he has a part-time job working in a home improvement center which is "beneath" him.

Anxiety is a *big* problem. He refused to make eye contact with strangers (anyone outside his immediate family) until he was five. We allowed him to take his time and didn't force it. Now he appears very polite with new people but it is all an act to cover up the anxiety. A very *good* act, by the way. He could be a stand-up comedian. He has always been funny beyond his years. When he was little, we were either laughing at his antics and impersonations or ready to kill him. Never in between. Oh, unless he had a fever of 105. Then he was so normal it was scary. He was concerned about others, empathetic, kind, understanding, gentle. Very strange – one doctor suggested that since neurotransmitters react in an enzyme environment, and since enzymes are heat sensitive, this phenomenon should be researched. My sister suggested we just put C's head in a microwave and see what happens! We have learned to laugh about a lot of things.

He believes that he knows more than anyone else. His facts are in separate cubby holes with no integration into what one would call "wisdom." He does have a remarkable memory, going back to when he was seventeen months old. He loves the History Channel and absorbs facts by osmosis. Reading is too slow but he loves documentaries. He tends to have one passion/interest at a time. When he was four, he worked puzzles for three months – his only activity at his preschool. Fortunately, we had a wonderfully creative, child-centered preschool where the teachers let the children be themselves. So for three months he did all the puzzles. After that, he moved to big blocks. And so on.

Etc. etc. etc....and now today...

Our biggest problems are dealing with his insensitivity. His four-year-old son asked me to talk to his daddy because his daddy tickles too hard and doesn't know that the game (played with us after work) doesn't involve tickling. He insults people and has no idea why they are angry. He is verbally cruel to his ex and can't imagine why people think so. "I only say the truth."

Another problem is his anxiety level. He is trying Paxil and it seems to help. He reacts to anxiety with anger. It's very hard to help him out. We feel that we are being attacked by someone who desparately wants us to help him. Talk about biting the hand that feeds you!

The other problem is his future. We have been supporting him and taking care of his ex while she got a degree and taking care of his son (who fortunately seems to have none of C's behaviors, although maybe some ADD characteristics). C has no insurance and we have to cover all his medical bills. He wants a career and prestige (in his mind, that can only be done with a college degree and lead to lots of money); we would be happy if he could just keep a job and maintain medical benefits. If he had money, he wouldn't have it long. He seems to have no sense of money management. If money is in his pocket, he spends it.

With his last paycheck, he said he needed clothes (he always needs clothes, partly because they are destroyed – holes, stains, tears – but also because he doesn't remember that the deep pile in his closet floor *is* his clothes). I said, "Be sure to keep enough money for your expenses for the next two weeks." He pays for his food and gasoline and incidentals. Last night, four days after pay day, he said, "I need to borrow some money." (That word means "have" ...he can never pay back anything.) It turns out he spent all his paycheck on clothes and has two dollars left to last ten days. His reasoning: "But I needed clothes. You have clothes. Why can't I have clothes? Just loan me some money." When I explained to him that I told him specifically not to buy clothes with all his money and to keep enough for food and gasoline, he said, "But I didn't spend all of it. I have two dollars left!" He would sound like a spoiled brat if you didn't hear his reasoning, or an eight year old. He has no clue why I was not happy with him. The doctor who diagnosed "psychotic aspects" when he was sixteen referred to his slightly askew way of thinking. It's not truly psychotic – no hallucinations, no voices, no elephants in his bedroom. It "sounds" reasonable if you don't listen very closely or know the truth. His thoughts just don't connect in the same paths that would be thought of as normal.

His relationship to our money is frightening. We worry about our financial future. He would take everything we have and then be mad if we couldn't give him more. His attitude never seems to mature. Immaturity is too mild a term for it. It really is bizarre.

Looking at his future and our future is overwhelming at this moment. I don't know how to survive a lifetime of these challenges without help. Surely there is someone somewhere who has some answers for how to help him so that he makes progress. If the next twelve years are like the last twelve, God help us all.

His sister is twenty-six and finishing law school. We are glad to have a lawyer in the family. At least his legal fees should be easier. That's a whole other chapter. He seems to be in the best place he has been in yet but we are so far from his being an independent, self-actualizing person. Without a good therapist to help us manage him, I don't know how things can ever change. And we can't stand for them to go on.

We have loving family and supportive friends, and they have some idea about what C is like but, still, they can't imagine what we go through on a daily basis.

*E.G., USA, 2002*

## 10

# A Commentary

I am married to a passive, silent man. He has never abused me physically or verbally (by this I mean swear or call me names). I don't believe I would have stayed if that was the case. He never ever gets angry, but at the same time he is never joyful or excited about anything. There is no range of feelings, always calm and non-reactive. The kids don't call when we are sick (most of the time they don't know, but even when they do) or on a special birthdays (never mind the rest of the year), and I ask him if he minds, he would answer quite flatly, "not really." He never, never looks anybody in the eye. I used to say, "look at me, look at me." He would try to look up and immediately look down – I saw a true physical pain on the contours of his face. For many years I believed he was not as good or kind as he seemed, because he was different from anybody I knew; I began to believe he was a true passive-aggressive in the worst sense, and was devastated by the punishment meted to me, an unbearable loneliness which I didn't feel I deserved. He is, I must add, a graduate of a prestigious university, a man of high verbal skills (though never able to express, in words, any emotions or feelings –

never), but ask him about some historical event and he can go on and on, not hearing anyone who interjects; I had been calling it "rolling down the hill," unable to stop, oblivious to what others have said or want to say. He is completely not in touch even with his own feelings, even concerning himself; cannot describe to a doctor how he feels physically, where he hurts. In general doesn't feel the difference between cold and hot. When he tightens the lid on a jar it is never closed; it is as if there is something wrong with his nerve ends – he doesn't feel it is still loose. He cannot hang his slacks, because he doesn't see or feel where the seams are, and cannot fold them. He cannot fold a sheet, unable to put four corners together. On the other hand if you touch him, he gets so startled and frightened and can jump out of the chair. We can drive for a whole day and he will not utter a word. He has a problem (now I believe it might be neurological) with doing two things at the same time; if he eats he cannot watch TV, or for that matter pay attention to what is said to him. If he is asked to take something with him when he goes out, he cannot do another thing besides that first one he was focused on. On the phone, in no way can you ask him to add additional information to what he was saying; he cannot handle double information at the same time. To be humorous (with tears in my eyes) he "cannot walk and chew gum." If I feel down, and tell him that (so he doesn't need to guess), he never touches me, or hugs me; he continues to do whatever he is doing; he cannot extend any emotional support, in word or deed. Whenever I ask a question dealing with the English language, the answer immediately is "I don't know." Now, that is impossible in real terms as English was his major and is what he knows upside down – it is my second language – he seems frightened, as if he is tested, a paranoia extended to all social skills. Very stressed, panicky, with making a phone call to a benign party, like a store, phone company, etc. No curiosity about anything, never wanting to travel, get out of familiar surroundings; I used to call it "feel stuck in cement" and on and on.

Now to the children (ranging in age from forty to fifty). My late father once said about them, when they were quite small, "Just like their father" (and he liked their father a great deal; he thought he was so kind, never losing his temper, or raising his voice). He was, of course, referring to the fact that they were not very affectionate, not at all like my warm, outgoing family. One of them was quite a happy smiling child, and I thought, Wow, maybe I am not just a vessel after all, just carrying my husband's genetic blueprint – I was wrong. All three are frightened of contact; all moved away. All bright, having been good students and I thought wonderful children, sort of quiet, not too many friends, outside of the one I had some hope for. I once wrote a letter to my eldest adult child, after his paternal grandmother died, and he said, because coming to the funeral would not help her, he wasn't coming. I wrote to him that his reactions were odd, never happy on an occasion such as his wedding, or other happy milestones, and never sad at losses. I didn't realize I was describing a syndrome. I used to think he was just withdrawn. I have not been successful in connecting with him, at all. He only wrote angry letters, warning not to come see him, disappeared from the horizon for years. He hasn't talked to us or been in contact for the last twenty-five years. It was so hard to understand how love and warmth begot hate and alienation. The others have some contact, but never utter what for them seem to be the hardest words: Dad or Mom. When they write, it is without greetings, and when we are together, on rare occasions, they move to another room, start reading when you talk to them, or walk away in the middle of a conversation. If you ask the simplest of question, like, how was the movie, the answer is "Why do you want to know?"

I could write a book, but I have said enough, more than I ever did, even to the closest of friends. *And*, it is truly a drop, not in the bucket, but in the ocean.

*Anonymous, USA, 2000*

*11*

# A Failed Marriage

Lower your eyes
Look away
Don't speak
Don't say the words

Ignore the pain
Suppress the hurt
Hide the tears

Bite your lip
Bite your tongue
Clench your teeth

Smile

Cry alone
Taste the bitterness
Don't show the scars

Don't let the raw wounds show
Bandages don't stem the flow
Bleed your pain away
In silence and loneliness

"Count your blessings" they say
What are they?
Work? Friends?
I had those before
God alone knows

Where are the soaring heights of joy?
Quiet content in shared lives?
Pleasure that comes from working as one
Single minded in intent?
Where the give and take of tolerance, respect?
The unselfish impulse that puts the other first?

Gone – soured like yesterday's milk left out in the
    sun
What did those words mean to you?
Did you stop to think?

And what of the future?
Cynicism?
Resentment?
Thinking the worst?
Is this all there is for me now?

No hope
No love
No protection

Be strong
Build your defences
Shut him out
Don't leave one chink for him to get through

\*\*\*

Isolation in the one relationship
Isolation from other's lives
Always on the outside
Watching
Listening
Trying to find the sense in it all

Nose pressed up against the glass of truth
Viewing, observing, analysing, describing
Keeps emotions at bay
And thought of what might have been

Can anyone touch me now
Can I be got at
Can I be hurt

I am an automaton
Without feelings
I do what I have to
To survive my existence

But I look and wonder and think at times

*Anonymous*

## 12

# Asperger's Syndrome, Obsessions, etc.

When our son was four years old, my husband and I were beginning to look into why he was so obviously different than other children his age, and had always seemed so to me. My husband was not aware of these differences on his own, but would not disagree when I would point them out to him. Remembering when our son was a baby and needed to be swaddled tightly in order to relax, someone recalled a documentary about Temple Grandin and her "squeeze box." This led us to the Internet, researching autism. My husband came to me one night, in tears, with pages he had printed out from an autism website, describing something called "Asperger's Syndrome." As he handed them to me, he said, "This explains my whole life!" As I read the numerous pages, I could see that the descriptions fit perfectly for both my son and my husband. We took our son to the leading autism doctor at Stanford University and, after extensive evaluation, he was formally diagnosed with Asperger's Syndrome. My husband is undiagnosed at this time; however, all of the professionals we have been to in order to assist our son have informally agreed that my husband apparently does have AS. The psychiatrist he is presently seeing has also not refuted this claim. We also believe that his mother has it, and he believes that her father and a brother of hers also probably had AS. His nephew has a severely autistic daughter.

This having been said, I will attempt to describe what living with a spouse with probable Asperger's Syndrome is like for me. When I first met my husband, we were both in the twelve-step program of Overeater's Anonymous. We both had struggled with obesity our entire lives and were successfully changing our lives working this spiritual program. We went with a group of people to the movies and that is how we first spent time together. Later, he and I and another person went to the movies again and, as he later told me, he was so taken with how much I enjoyed the film and laughed so freely that he asked me for a date as we walked to our cars. We agreed to meet in a week's time at a restaurant. I remember thinking this was odd that he didn't offer to pick me up at my apartment, but since we were going to a play after dinner and it was nearer to his place, I put it down to this. He was recently separated from his wife of three years and was living in an apartment of his own. We began seeing each other frequently and, although he seemed "different" (socially awkward) to me, I put this down to the fact that he was from England and that he was just not one of the dangerous losers I seemed to hook up with. He had a good job as a software engineer, a very nice apartment; he was very intelligent, kind, funny and interesting and, most important, he was very interested in me. He was reliable and dependable; always showing up when he said he would. I had never had a man so attentive to me. My lack of self-esteem had caused me to date (and sometimes only sleep with) anyone who showed any interest in me. I had been working on changing this in my life, and he seemed like the fruits of that labor. He acquired his divorce several months later and moved in with me. Fortunately, he had no children with his ex-wife.

We lived together for three years and were then married in a beautiful wedding. Our son was born two years later and that is when I started noticing changes in my husband. The company he was running went under and he was jobless. He was depressed, but not alarmingly so. His love for our son was obvious, but I noticed that, although he wasn't afraid to take care of him, he would get stymied if the first remedy for crying didn't work, and would just keep on doing the only thing he could think of, despite the fact that the crying would escalate. He seemed increasingly detached from us and isolated himself from social situations. He would talk to me in long monologues on subjects he had spoken about frequently. I noticed that he would say, for example, "I was just thinking," and then launch into a story or information he had told me countless times. Other times he would say, "I know I've told you this millions of times before," then tell me something he had never told me. He rarely asked me a question about something I was relating to him, but would ask the same questions about the same stories he was telling me. I could tell he wasn't really interested in listening to what I had to say because most times he would interrupt me and change the subject completely. In social situations, he would look like he was in a world of his own, and would not make eye contact with anyone other than me. His eye contact with me has always been uncomfortable for me as it goes beyond the limit of those natural "rules" that most people instinctively know. He has extreme "face blindness" and cannot identify people as familiar unless he has seen them frequently and can remember a particular detail about them. This leads to embarrassment when he obviously doesn't recognize someone saying hello to him and looks blankly at him or her, or doesn't look at them at all. He has often said that I'm his interpreter of social cues and, when at a party, he'll talk to me almost exclusively.

After ten years of marriage, I've learned to live with these foibles and now that we know about Asperger's Syndrome, it has helped me immensely to not feel angry about certain aspects of our relationship. I can see that he truly doesn't understand my feelings sometimes, and even though I explain them to him, he just can not understand if he hasn't experienced them himself. He is very involved with helping our son, but relates to his problems with AS only as they have affected himself, unable to understand that our son has a different life and different strengths and weaknesses and experiences. All in all, until the past few months, I would classify our marriage as successful, even with some problems.

In the two years leading up to the year 2000, he became completely obsessed with preparing for the "catastrophe." Besides talking endlessly about it at every chance, he began stocking our garage with canned food and purchased an expensive diesel generator. Every conversation with him eventually wound up with Y2K. He kept up fanatically with all the news and every chat group on the Internet. He took money out of the bank and purchased gold with it. He was so wrapped up in talking about it that I dreaded when company came over or we went to someone's house because he would keep bringing the conversation around to this.

Recently, my husband had a heart attack and triple by-pass surgery. He had a very close brush with death and has changed his physical lifestyle tremendously. Unfortunately, after the first couple of weeks of feeling just so grateful to be alive, he was plunged into a serious, suicidal depression. He has been plagued with memories from his early teenage years of the taunting and physical abuse that he suffered from other kids. He had been institutionalized for depression and was treated with several electroshock therapy sessions. He remembered being unable to write adequately until he was eleven years old. And he revealed to me for the first time that he was a cross-dresser. In trying to work out our relationship in view of this, his inability to understand someone else's feelings is shown most dramatically. He told me that he can't understand why this would be such a big deal for me. He is unwilling to provide me with information about the extent to which he practices this obsession and what he plans to do in the future. His comment was, "it's like if I told you I was going fishing...would I need to tell you what kind of bait I would be using?"

He feels very sad that our son cannot know the "real" him and honestly believes that this eight year old would understand. He doesn't understand why I don't wish to have physical intimacy with him now. He wants to discuss this and has started quoting stories or news items about "trans-genderism" whenever possible. It is the same cycle as the Y2K obsession. It is the same cycle of obsession as our son's Game Boy and Pokemon monologues. I feel like I have been robbed. Although my husband and our son are very high functioning, there is a whole depth of life with them that I'll never have. I feel for him sincerely…I can imagine the pain he suffered all of his life. He is a good man who has had to compensate for a lack of understanding of how his brain works. I plan to give our son as much help as I can so that he doesn't have to experience this kind of pain. Whether or not my husband and I can work out our problems and maintain our marriage, I can't say at this time.

*Anonymous, USA, 2000*

## Update

It's been interesting to read my original contribution to *The Book of FAAAS* and see how much has taken place in two years since then.

Shortly after submitting my essay, my husband received a diagnosis of Asperger's Syndrome. Athough he'd concluded long before the diagnosis that he probably did have AS, after seeing a specialist at Stanford University, who is one of the only doctors in our area who will evaluate adults, he questioned "whether this doctor knew what he was doing" – "they're all useless these mental health professionals."

A tremendous event for me after submitting my contribution to the book was attending the first ever FAAAS Inc. Conference in Cape Cod, MA. Although I'd been a member of the FAAAS listserve for a while, meeting in person with these wonderful people who made such an impact on my life, and being able to spend hours listening and talking one on one with others who understood first-hand the challenges of living with a spouse with Asperger, was such a gift. The main speaker was Tony Attwood, who I'd heard on several occasions in conjunction with Asperger in children (but was also the person from whom I first heard of FAAAS!). This time, though, he was discussing the impact on the families and he really "got it"; he knew what he was talking about and he was the first professional who I'd ever heard acknowledge the challenges and difficulties without mincing words and trying to minimize and placate us. When we broke into discussion groups, the group focusing on partners was so large that we went around and each person brought up an issue that was a factor in their relationship with an adult with AS. Almost everything that was listed I could relate to and some things just hit me in the solar plexus because they explained feelings I'd had all these years and just thought it was me; that I was imagining things or I was being too dramatic.

One person in the group said the first thing that started the changes in my life: "leaving a partner with Asperger would feel like abandoning a handicapped child." I realized that my issue was "Then how does one have an intimate, fulfilling marital relationship with an adult that is, in essence, like one of your children?"

When it was time for the group to disperse and return to the presentation, Tony took a look at all the issues he'd written down which we'd literally poured out of our hearts, and quietly said, "You all deserve better."

In the year that followed the conference, my husband's obsession with issues of trans-genderism became all-consuming, even interfering with his ability to concentrate on work. He was self-employed at the time, and his business began to crumble. We sought couples counseling with therapists specializing in trans- genderism, but none of them knew about Asperger's Syndrome! If they'd even heard of it, they knew next to nothing about it, and certainly not in adults and how that impacts a marriage. The sessions became about helping us to stay together by setting boundaries, which were acceptable to me around his activities in pursuing this lifestyle. He was very quickly unable to honor these agreements, however. Someone unfamiliar with the power and focus of an Asperger obsession in day-to-day life cannot imagine how that affects the families. The financial impact alone is tremendous, but the emotional toll is much greater, especially when that obsession is something not widely accepted socially.

Eventually, my husband began making decisions on his own, which seriously involved the future of our family. When I would find out, his explanation was, "it's easier to beg forgiveness than to ask permission." For me, this was painful on two levels: he's doing something that he knows I have strong feelings against without giving me an opportunity to voice my concerns; and he feels he has to ask my permission? I was already struggling with the issues of feeling like I was his mother.

We tried to figure out a way that we could stay together for the sake of our son, but I had reached a point where I no longer trusted him, and I felt myself slipping into depression. I realized that one of us needed to be there for our son, and it wasn't going to be him. I moved out of our house because I knew that my husband was in no shape to do that and I just had to be away from the chaos before it suffocated me.

We have been separated now for over a year and have just filed for divorce. What I have learned in this year is that in order to keep things amicable and running smoothly, I must continue on some level to take care of him, gradually pulling away one area at a time so he's able to handle the change and adjust. I've had to make decisions about which issues truly matter to me rather than just needing to be the one who is "right." I've also had to set boundaries and speak up about what is no longer comfortable for me, such as kissing and intimate touches.

Recently, someone on the FAAAS listserve wrote that she sees that she's set up this "scaffolding" to hold her husband up and help him along. In going through separation with an adult with Asperger's Syndrome, I've had to realize that I can't just pull that scaffolding away abruptly because the structure could fall and, more than likely, it would fall on me and our son. So much of the world of people is confusing to people with AS, and their struggle is to try to control that which they don't understand. That control can sometimes lead to violence, as they are unable to adapt to the situation. In my experience, it's been beneficial to continue to relate to my husband with as much love and respect as I can and to provide some of that "scaffolding" where it really will help to keep him strong. This is especially important for our son because, with him also having Asperger, that stability is even more crucial.

I still feel that my husband is an extraordinary person who has had to deal with more than I can possibly imagine in his lifetime, and has come through it as a decent, loving, caring individual. I told him a few months into our separation that I could not be with him anymore because I didn't want to begin to hate him; I wanted to continue to respect and love him as my friend and as the father of our son.

*Anonymous, USA, 2002*

*13*

# Naked Hands

Naked hands

Flaunt their tan lines.
Flirt with entanglements.
Tap dance on tabletops.

Naked hands

Visit neglected temples.
Explore abandoned caves.
Pick at old wounds.
Wipe away futile tears.

Naked hands

Steepled in prayer,
Give thanks for the simple joys of
Thumbness and pinkiehood.

*Kathy Read, USA, 2002*

*14*

# Personal Reflections on a Relationship with an Adult who has the Symptoms of Asperger's Syndrome

Three years ago, in 1997, I learned how to use the Internet. The first thing I looked up was high functioning autism, the subcategory – Asperger's Syndrome. I was truly amazed to read in that description of the syndrome, not my autistic two-year-old's behaviors, but rather every problem behavior I had ever had with my husband. This revelation changed me and the way I viewed my husband and the way I viewed our relationship.

I used to think he was very immature in his behavior and emotions. I used to warn my friends, before I introduced him to them, that he was a little slow but a really nice and smart guy. He seems slow because he often has long pauses between his words where I can think of a whole paragraph of words during the time space it takes him to finish a sentence. Other times he will speak at a regular speed but very loud. He seemed unique in that he didn't have much concept of mechanical things and in many situations he didn't seem to have much sense of logic. I often thought he was really mean to me and that he tried to hurt me by lying to me and by being so withdrawn. There was so much I didn't understand, but reading this description of Asperger gave the complete picture of him and if nothing else it gave me great insight to our situation.

When I met him in college, he spoke out in class knowing the subject material thoroughly. He was impressive with the details and the way he added humor to the dialog. He is a handsome man, a strong build from playing soccer in his youth. He looks outgoing and adventurous in his appearance. He seemed, in the classroom context, a perfect candidate for a mate. But then in seeing him in his apartment, in his own space, there was a different person. His place was a wreck and so was he. He was severely depressed and introverted. He would make commitments but never follow through. Like he would tell me he would call or come over and I would expect him, but he would never show up. He did the same with his college advisors, set an appointment but later call with a lame excuse like he had a flat tire. He really knows the right answer to situations and can say the right thing, but just doesn't follow through on them. He also had a gambling problem and would lose his rent money and have to borrow money from people, other students or finagle his parents. This demonstrated his ability to manipulate others. I felt sorry for him and felt that all he needed was some love and support and he would be a decent guy. He seemed dependent on me for support and talked of suicidal feelings. I felt secure in the relationship and that I would be able to help him overcome his sadness. We dated for a year and decided we would like to have a family together.

It has been ten years now and we have three sons, and now I too suffer depression. Because he is a picky eater, he will eat hardly anything I cook; however, he enjoys cooking for the family. Because he is a sensitive and loud sleeper, he sleeps in his own room. We have never had any romance as he finds the idea appalling. We do not make love – we have sex. We never go out. He has very rarely bought me (or anyone else) any gifts for any occasion, only when pressured by me. I usually buy my own birthday gift and have him wrap it. His gambling addiction continues to ruin my life. I quit working as an editor because he lost more money than I brought home. We have no financial security and I must play bank-card keeper to try to thwart his compulsive behavior. He gets upset when I am happy so I have learned to be subdued in his presence. He is a natural kill-joy. He is only nice to me when I am very upset. I think it is his need to control his situation. He seems to need me to play the part of his mother and reprimand him when he is bad. He is indeed a strain on me similar to having to take care of an overgrown adolescent.

He is a fairly good father to our three sons. He will do anything they ask him too. If I tell my older son to put his garbage in the trash can, my husband will jump up and do it for him. Other times, especially on the weekends when he starts drinking beer in the morning, he becomes quite threatening to all of us and we try to keep our distance from him. He has a short temper and lacks common sense. He has a hard time with simple mechanics. He is an excellent scientist and finely specialized. He holds a high technical position and is near the top salary range in his field. Promotions in his work have greatly enhanced his level of responsibility and self-esteem. I believe he is very loyal to me as far as extramarital affairs go, and I think he does not want us to break up.

After learning about Asperger's, I now honestly think he doesn't do anything to purposely hurt me. He doesn't know he hurts me even though I have tried to explain it to him hundreds of times. Understanding Asperger's, to the degree available today, makes the whole situation rational and provides better logic for dealing with the situations. It has given me relief from suffering and fighting for things I wanted. Now I know I will never get certain things from him – a deeper love, support, understanding, comradeship, or romance. I know he will always lie to me because that is the only way he knows to handle the situation. I know he will always try to control me and keep me down, despite also wanting me to be happy. I have read that other people have been successful at "training" their Asperger spouses using appropriate motivational techniques. These techniques will be very beneficial in the future as more people are made aware of this syndrome.

He had difficulties as a child, when learning disabilities were rarely recognized. He was a constant disappointment to his father and the only people who would hang out with him were there just to take advantage of him. He had no real friends. He would get in trouble to get attention. This defined his identity; he probably has never known support and acceptance, only ridicule and criticism. This is how he was molded and this is the only way he knows. It is hard to teach people with Asperger's new concepts; I think they seemed to have stopped maturing quite early and retained an adolescent or younger mentality. I think extra caution should be taken with ADD and Asperger's Syndrome children, to keep them in a positive supportive environment, free from teasing and belittlement, otherwise they will have a hard time dealing with relationships for the rest of their lives. They can take their time in learning their few pet subjects; this part nearly always evolves on its own. But early support in relationships seems crucial to their getting along in the workplace and ever maintaining a long-term relationship.

I still hold out hope that there is a biological cause for this behavior. One of our sons appears to also be afflicted with this syndrome. I have noticed things like removing dairy from his diet greatly improved his behavior. I have not been successful in manipulating my husband's diet. From the vast amounts of information I have read seeking answers to my other son's autism, I believe it is quite possible that an infection such as a streptococcal strain may be responsible for some of these behaviors and other factors such as diet may enhance these problems.

Getting a valid diagnosis for my husband might be beneficial. I made him read about it that very first day I read about it. He did not ever want to read more about autism again after that day. The implications are quite threatening to him. Is he responsible for our children's problems? Is he really different and handicapped compared to normal people? What if his co-workers found out; would it hurt his opportunity for advancement? What would his parents say? What if I divorced him; would he get any custody of the kids? He absolutely did not want anything more to do with this subject, but I think it would be great if he could get some behavior workshops and therapy and medication if needed to help with his depression and anxiety.

*Anonymous, USA, 2000*

# 15

# When We Married

When we married, we both assumed that our partner
would have the same view of married life

When we married, I thought that problems could be
worked out by talking and explaining my views

When we married, I thought your love for me would
overcome your tendency towards selfishness

When we married, I thought you would listen to my
opinions and advice

When we married, I thought we both wanted a
family

When we married, I thought that as long as we were
both working, there would be a fair division of
household tasks and that we would do things for
each other out of love

When we married, I thought that we would have a
social life, shared friends, time to enjoy ourselves,
doing the things we both enjoyed doing and
enjoying each other's hobbies as well

When we married, I thought that I would have more
choice over furniture and room arrangements

When we married, I thought that we would be open with each other over our financial situation

When we married, I thought we would develop our own routines and a lifestyle which enabled us to discuss the day-to-day events of our lives equally

When we married, I thought we would be open with one another, with no secrets and that any rules we had would be shared and jointly agreed

When we married, I thought that we would decide important things together

When we married, I thought we would continue going to church together

When we married, I thought we would have a close physical relationship


When we married, I thought you would compliment me, notice the trouble I took and the efforts I made

When we married, I thought you would realize that I sometimes needed support and encouragement

When we married, I thought you would understand my need for some space to call my own

When we married, I thought that I only had to ask you to do something once or twice for it to be done

When we married, I thought you had a good sense of direction and could find your way to places you had been to before

When we married, I wanted nothing more than to make you happy and to be made happy by you

Now I want nothing more than to be left alone

I have no hope that anything will ever change

I see no point in talking. It tires me out and makes
me ill

We can come to a workable arrangement

Provided neither of us has any expectation that the
other will ever do anything of any practical help
or support

I will look after myself. You will look after yourself

I do not expect you to cook for me, wash or iron my
clothes or tidy up after me

Any favours we do for each other are to be done
without any expectation of reciprocation

I don't expect you to be interested in my work, my
friends, my hobbies or any other aspect of my life

I do expect you to keep me informed about your
diary and to tell me anything I need to know
about our financial situation

I want no more rows, or arguments

I don't want you to try to change my point of view

Don't make comments starting with "if I were you'

Don't suggest that what I am doing is wrong or not
good enough

Our lives are incompatible

Trying to find some way to manage our relationship
has made me ill

I do not have the energy or stamina to continue
trying

Neither do I have any desire to try

You have beaten me

Congratulations

*Anonymous, 2001*

*16*

# When Cassandra was Very, Very Young

Where to begin telling a story that is age old, and yet has never been told, or not in the last century or so, and I should know because I've been combing the libraries of the world ever since I could read to find a precedent.

There are glimpses of it in myth and fairy tale, but it has not seen the light of day since Freud kicked off the psycho-analytical revolution, and with his followers set in stone all the categories by which we came to understand what it is to be human.

This is the story of the singular hell of growing up with a "parent" with a kind of mind that was never dreamed of in any psychotherapy, a kind of mind that nobody believed existed. Except, as far as I knew, me, when I was four, maybe five, years old.

I may not have had the words, but I knew in my bones that there were two kinds of people in the world: the people who were...just right, who somehow innately "clicked", and then there was my mother. Or so the people called this strange, mewling entity who sometimes hovered over my cot-world and never failed to set it on edge.

Later on, when I was eight or nine, as I struggled to define the mystery of my mother's peculiar "otherness", I puzzled to myself: "It's as if she dropped into our world from a parallel universe, almost the same as ours, but tantalizingly, indefinably different."

Here's my earliest memory of my mother, surely singled out because it was the tip of the iceberg of so many pre-verbal incidents. And it certainly set the blue-print for the rest of my childhood.

I was no more than five years old, and defending my father from one of my mother's "hysterical" tantrums. "Hysterical" was clearly a word I had heard early and often. In a harsh and unnatural screech that scraped my nerves raw, she was screaming that it was all my father's fault that the coffee cup was broken and the coffee spilled, although we all knew he wasn't in the room when she dropped it.

My father was remonstrating desperately against an irrefutable illogic, but I was beside myself with the injustice of it, and determined that she had to be made to admit the truth. And I felt so sad for my father, who already seemed somehow crushed, hopeless, drowned.

In case you're wondering whether I got it wrong – how could a five-year-old remember that; everyone knows that children are unreliable witnesses – it's easy to date my memories, because we emigrated to Australia when I was five, and this scene was set in my parents' room back in the European apartment.

There I go again, offering careful proof, a watertight case, as if I were before a court, fighting for my life, or rather fighting to prove that my mother was the source of the problem, not me, so please don't hang me for being the one who raised the issue.

Well, the issue wasn't in the textbooks; the psychiatrists had never heard of it.

Therefore, it didn't exist.

And we all know what happened back then in the 1950s and 1960s to anyone who admitted to varieties of experience that weren't itemized in the psychiatric textbooks.

And we didn't want to go there.

So I think it's easy enough to understand why there was an urgency to my case.

But I'm going to give myself a break, and take it on trust that, thanks to the burgeoning AS movement, it's safe to speak out here, that it's not me and my credibility that is on trial, that the mass of evidence is now out there, and that the tide for us, the children of people with AS, is turning.

I'm going to trust that some of you will believe me, even if I don't succeed in pre-empting every skeptical question you may have, or in reconciling every contradiction on these few pages.

I wish I had the space to write more about what my mother was like – I am bursting with a story that is desperate to emerge but it will take many volumes and many voices other than my own to get it out there.

Well, I'll say just this much: my mother was a classic AS woman, the effusive, not withdrawn, kind. Yes, she drove me absolutely crazy. Yes, it derailed my life, drained my energies, and my life is only just now beginning, at fifty.

It's a complex and subtle story, there's no simple formula to it, and the villain of the piece keeps shifting:

– from my wicked mother for relentlessly tormenting me with the egocentricity, the jaw-droppingly unbelievable selfishness with her endless, repetitive, inane questioning, the same questions, day after day, despite my begging and pleading – no, please don't ask me the same questions again, can't you see how much it hurts me, for pity's sake look at my face, can't you see? – with the excruciating social embarrassment when others copped the questioning and the interminable monologues on her one pet topic, the alternate raging and suffocating clinging dependency of an infant-in-an-adult's-clothing but, worst of all, for her constant abuse of my loving, giving, generous, wonderful father

– to my broken-spirited father who, inexplicably, allowed himself bit by bit to be sucked dry, though I *told* him and *told* him can't you see that she's crazy, don't let her do this to you, take her to a psychiatrist, divorce her, save us from this relentless mental water-torture, who, in one horrific night of betrayal, showed me that he would rather see me drugged or dead rather than face up to what he had allowed himself to become

– to the mental health apparatchiks of the 1950s and 1960s who, in their ignorance, and arrogance, thought they had the field covered. If he had succumbed to their "help" what options were there? Either he would have been disbelieved and blamed, or he would have seen my mother (who he loved, whose welfare he was devoted to, however inexplicable I found it) diagnosed as schizophrenic, and slowly destroyed in one of the horror hospitals of the era

– to the legal system who I knew would have awarded custody to my mother, who wouldn't have asked me my opinion of which parent I wanted, so that I lived in terror of being taken away from my father into bedlam with her, so that I lived with the knowledge that he sacrificed himself to save me

– to myself for what I had done or not done, for not parenting my parents better.

Of course we all know that there is no villain, only lack of awareness. We are a young species, still evolving, still learning about ourselves. Who knew? Who could blame us?

But once this gets around, there will be no more excuses. OK, that's already more than I wanted to say. I'm going to cut to the quick here.

FAAAS' constituency are partners of people with AS, so it is to this audience, and to those who would help them, that I want to address myself.

The worst part of having an AS family was not actually my mother's behavior. She was a nuisance, a pest who wouldn't give me a moment's peace. But it didn't cut to the core. She didn't really count, because the presence, the consciousness that would have counted, was not there.

She was simply a black hole, down which everything disappeared forever. I could always get some semblance of relief by yelling at her to try using her brains for once in her life, and I knew she had them, or how else could she have topped her year at university in an era when most women never even dreamt of going there?

No, the worst part was my father's denial, the murderous pressure he put on me to pretend that we were a normal family, so that I lived in fear of giving away the "family secret". I understand now the social background to what he did. That background has got to be changed forever. It is changing now.

So please don't deny the truth when your children try to tell you that they know. Mourn the years you have already wasted, because you cannot have them back, but don't send any more good years after the bad. Don't try to keep a lid on your pain by silencing your children. That's all they want. The truth. They will make their own way with the AS parent once they know they are not alone. You will be all right in the end, though it will not be painless.

I want to finish with a paradox, the paradox of AS, at least in women, which is what I know best.

After all that I have said about there not being a consciousness there, I must now contradict myself completely.

Actually I have always known that my mother loves me deeply.

And I know that she "knows" me in the deepest sense there is.

This consciousness is not available to her in her day-to-day existence, but we both know it underlies everything.

She knows that I am good and brave and strong and wise, and she knows that I have held her in trust, that one day I would work out what it was that caused our family so much suffering, that one day I would make everything all right.

And I was determined to survive, and determined to figure it out, determined to make sure that no child would ever be left alone, disbelieved, unsupported, invalidated in the way that I was.

I am so proud that, at nearly fifty, my life really began, in ways I could never have imagined, when I started the world's first support group for people who tentatively thought they might have been raised by a parent on the autistic spectrum.

I will never forget, as I set up ASpar, my e-group, waiting to see who was out there, knowing now for sure that there must be so many of us, all thinking we were alone, and wondering if we would recognize each other when we met.

And, reader, we did.

We child Cassandras have grown up somehow and found each other. We have so much to teach the world when our collective voice grows to a volume that can no longer be ignored!

*Judy Singer, Australia, 2002*

*17*

# Roses and Cacti

I see people with Asperger's Syndrome (aspies) as cacti, which are soft and vulnerable inside – but very soon in life they develop very cruel prickles to protect themselves from painful contacts with neurotypicals (NTs). Aspies belong in the desert. They are happy there. Occasionally they bloom – and it is so wonderful they light up the whole desert - but it is short-lived. Being natives of the desert they have the ability to withstand long periods of drought. When water is available they absorb it quickly and store it in their fleshy stems for times of need.

Cacti have a right to be cacti, and to live in the desert, and to have prickles.

I see neurotypicals as roses. The roots of roses must not be allowed to dry out. They need to be in a rose garden where they can constantly connect with other roses and be watered, fed and mulched. They need to be protected from the fierce heat of the desert and from shredding desert sandstorms. Most roses do not survive in the desert. The ones that do mostly become stunted, lose their flowers, develop larger ugly thorns, move into denial and often need medication. Medicated roses no longer see the harshness of the desert.

When the rose begins to wilt and tries to explain to the cactus that it needs rose food, the cactus will look out from the comfort of its stored reserves and ignore the rose. This is a form of passive aggression. As the rose's needs become desperate and the rose becomes increasingly demanding, the cactus can escalate to mental and emotional abuse in his lack of understanding of the rose's needs. The cactus does not mind if others are present – adding public humiliation to his abuse of the rose. When the pain of deprivation takes the rose beyond the boundaries of caution and reason, the cactus may escalate to door-slamming and physical abuse. The abused, starving rose retreats and grows a little more stunted and ugly.

Aspies do not understand that roses need rose food (emotional connection, tender loving care, appreciation, communication, time out for chatting complete with an emotional component, understanding, romance, etc.). Cactus food cannot nourish, or even sustain, a rose.

Aspies can only provide cactus food. When the rose begins to wilt and tries to explain that it needs rose food, the cactus will not understand and may call the rose "selfish" and "ungrateful". In the desert, with a prickly cactus, is a scary place for a rose to be. The rose will be deprived of intimate emotional connection, communication and love. Home-making will become a nightmare, because the cactus in his desert environment has no need for all the finishing touches that a rose would consider essential in her rose garden.

If a rose tries to bloom in the desert, the petals will be shredded by the merciless onslaught of the most ferocious desert sandstorms. In the process of desperately trying to provide myself with some mulch, water and food, I have mapped out a basic survival plan for a rose living in the desert with a cactus.

## Survival plan for roses

### 1. Encouragement

When I have any sort of a petal on my rose at all that has not been shredded in a recent sandstorm, I try to apply myself to encouraging and acknowledging the strengths in my aspie cactus.

The soft, vulnerable part of the aspie is very receptive to praise and compliments and appreciation (like we all are, but I have found them to be more so). He has many good points. The problem is that the cruel sandstorms and the empty spareness of the desert have so stunted and shredded the rose that is me, that mostly I cannot even enjoy the good points. Nevertheless, I have found that encouragement and appreciation cause him to bloom in a very special way.

### 2. Quick forgiveness

There will be no remorse or apologies on the part of the cactus, because it only sees that it has been unfairly attacked and that the rose is ungrateful and too demanding. Eventually the rose has to find a way to forgive and keep going. This is survival because bitterness only hurts the rose and the cactus won't notice whether the rose is bitter or not.

### 3. A whole-body exerciser

Some means of exhausting the physical body is pretty much an essential first-aid emergency treatment for the larger, cruel, shredding, searing desert sandstorms. The clue is to stay with the exercise until the tears come. This is exhausting but healing and needs to be followed by step four.

### 4. A good book and video

Roses need these as a first-aid measure to take the mind and emotions out of the desert and back into some sort of rose-garden environment.

### 5. Good friends

Understanding friends are the remedy for the loneliness and the isolation of the desert. The problem is, to have a good friend you have to be a good friend. That is a very difficult thing to do for a stunted, shredded rose who is unwell through humiliation and lack of rose food. Internet support groups like FAAAS can be life preserving and a privilege at times like this.

### 6. Telephone counseling services that run 24 hours a day

These are valuable for the desperate loneliness that hits around midnight and after. Just to hear another voice that is caring, accepting and non-judgmental does wonders.

### 7. Rose food

Roses have to supply their own. This is difficult when the cactus controls the budget and sees rose food as wasteful and extravagant. Gardening, reading, writing, painting, knitting, crocheting and loving chats with neighbours can often be invisibly worked into a desert budget.

## 8. Sleep

A cactus can be asleep within minutes of a desert sandstorm. A rose, however, will be hurting and desperate and may need to work through points three and four above.

## 9. Summary

The cactus is in the desert and easily survives the sandstorms. The rose cannot survive the shredding without lots of insight and protective measures on hand. Even then it is tough going!

## Regarding marriage

Cacti have areas of brilliance that become their obsessions. Common obsessions are computers, technology, engineering and religion. Sometimes a male aspie will turn his obsessive interests towards a female neurotypical.

A cactus in full bloom is magnificent and very difficult for a rose to resist. At this early stage of the relationship the rose has not experienced, or been shredded by, the desert sandstorms – and has not been stunted by the emptiness and lack of nurture and food. The early cactus bloom stage may last some time (particularly if there are no children and the rose is financially independent).

However, the rose is now in the desert – and the desert does not sustain it. The wilt is inevitable. I am sorry to have to say it.

Many of the neurotypical women most likely to end up married to aspies had aspie fathers so the awful feelings of abuse and loneliness seem normal to them and almost comfortable because these feelings are so familiar.

## Invisible wheelchairs

To a neurotypical, an aspie may seem emotionally disabled. Many people marry severely disabled people (such as quadriplegics) and with a lot of support and help manage to live reasonable lives. The difference here is that the quadriplegic knows he has the disability. Aspies mostly do not recognize their disability and mostly they judge the emotional interactions of neurotypical people as weakness and lack of self-discipline. Also, as you push around the quadriplegic's wheelchair people generally will make way for you, support you, even probably smile and affirm that you are doing a good job.

When a rose marries a cactus, the rose may come to feel that she is pushing an invisible wheelchair – on her own – without support and without help. People cannot "see" an invisible wheelchair, so the rose often may feel uncomfortable, even humiliated, when out in public with the cactus. In additon to this there may be a strong chance that offspring from this marriage could also be cacti. From the rose's perception – this amounts to more invisible wheelchairs.

## Raising baby cacti

It is my opinion that young aspie cacti need people of insight to go in to bat for them. They need a kindly advocate. They are soft and vulnerable and do not yet have their protective prickles established.

I believe that whenever possible the young aspie's obsessions or "special interests" (and they may change as they get older) need to be nurtured and supported. These special interests are often computing, engineering, mathematics and science.

If the young aspie can be led into earning a living from his area of "special interest", I believe he will be content and functional in his world as an adult.

It is my belief however, from observation and experience, that this state of contentment and stability will be completely destroyed if he chooses to marry a neurotypical.

I believe the different brain patterns in people with Asperger's Syndrome do not allow for functional social interaction except on a very surface, factual level. I believe the aspie can be trained to say the right things at the right time, but have found that does not supply the emotional connection that is necessary for intimate relationships with neurotypicals.

## Baby roses in the desert

Perhaps two cacti may exist happily together in the desert. However, think of the consequences of two cacti producing a baby rose. The baby rose, without any intention or effort from the cacti, would be subject to emotional deprivation and would be shredded in the desert. It is likely it would grow up stunted, without flowers and with very large thorns. Then it would look more like a cactus than a rose and would not fit into, or be accepted by, the rose garden.

Ultimately, the stunted, cactus-like rose would probably attract to itself another cactus rather than a rose. Unwittingly, then the rose would place itself in a marriage where all the pain, and more, of the rose's childhood would be revisited.

I wonder how many roses that are married to a cactus were in fact brought up by at least one cactus parent?

*18*

# Loneliness Is...

No one to care with
No one to share with
No one to talk with
No one to laugh with
No one to cry with
No one to love with
No one to listen
No one.

    I yearn for someone to talk to.
    Someone to share, to care,
    to laugh, to cry, to love with,
    To listen to the silence with.
    There is no one.

*Karen E. Rodman, USA, 1995*

# 19

# Bobby...

Hi, I would like to participate in this book. I have a family of a son Peter, thirty-three years old; a daughter Lisa, thirty years old; her son Al, who is thirteen years old and my grandchild; and there is Bobby, he is twenty-seven years old now.

When Bobby was born we all lived in New York. When my husband died in 1987 we had to move, so in 1988 we moved to Philadelphia. The thing I regret the most was moving to a city where there is no help and support if the person with special needs (at the time Bobby had been diagnosed with Pervasive Developmental Disorder) is living at home with his family. To get Bobby back into school, first I had to go back to NY to get his school and medical records, and when that wasn't enough I had to get a lawyer to find a school for him.

We found a private school, and at that school is where he met his best friend. He didn't miss his dad as much. This continued for about four years. Bobby helped his friend and his buddy helped him out – they were support for each other. This all came to an end when his best friend, his buddy, died from a brain aneurysm. That's when everything just got worse, the whole family suffered as well as Bobby. We didn't realize how much this friend meant to him...he was like a bridge to the outside world and when Bobby lost this friend he lost everything.

Bobby started to act like he was depressed and continued to act more depressed with each day that passed. There was a change in him that we could not handle. Every day was worse for him then than the day before. Bobby was going into meltdowns or rages every day. The mental health agency was no help. We went through every doctor. We were in crisis. The agency sent a behavior consultant and he told us about a seminar he went to, given by Tony Attwood. He told us about how PDD is linked to this thing called Asperger's Syndrome. He knew more about this than the doctors did at the agency. We tried talking to the director at the agency yet she was going by what the doctors were saying and not listening to us or the behavior consultant and things were getting worse. I tried calling the autism center to have a doctor see Bobby but couldn't get an appointment until two months from when I called.

With Bobby out of control by then, it just took its toll on me. I had to be hospitalized for hypertension. Nobody would listen to us when we went to the mental health agency. That's where we were supposed to go for help when we needed it. Hence the Cassandra thing happened again and again to us. He was having these meltdowns every day. I was too sick to help him so he wouldn't have these meltdowns. My daughter hurt her back when she tried to help him when he was having one of his meltdowns. It was getting obvious to us that he needed to be hospitalized, because the doctors couldn't figure out what kind of medication was needed to get him under control. The doctor at the mental health agency was treating Bobby for schizophrenia and there was no improvemnt, while the behavior consultant was saying he thought Bobby should be taking anti-depressant and not anti-psychotic medication.

On one medication he was like Jekyll and Hyde. On another medication he had tics like Tourettes. It went on and on. We took him to the emergency room when one of the medications caused him to have heart palpitations. We thought he was having a heart attack. We had to commit him to a psychiatric hospital. Bobby was there about three days when his blood pressure was taken in front of us. It was seventy over fifty. I thought he was going to die. That was the worst we ever saw him. The hospital was listening to the doctors at the mental health agency instead of to us and the behavior consultant.

The agency didn't even let the behavior consultant know that Bobby was in the hospital. When he found out, he became Bobby's advocate. We found out the doctors were treating him for schizophrenia. That's why he was getting worse after being there for ten days. They had him tied up and were giving him injections of Haldol. So as soon as a doctor was found who knew how to treat Bobby, and knew what medication he should be taking, he was getting better within a week. After twenty seven days he was well enough to come home.

On the day of Bobby's discharge both the behavior consultant and the director of the mental health agency were there. I made a determination that I would consult with the behavior consultant and he helped me connect with the doctor Bobby has now through the Autistic Society. What a difference it has been for him since the right diagnosis was made. The doctor at the Autistic Society confirmed Asperger's Syndrome. In Bobby's case, the right medication has made a difference, and this has happened only because we found the right doctor who knew what was wrong with him. It wasn't until the behavior consultant communicated with the doctor Bobby has now that things turned around for him and for us. When more people in the medical profession understand and recognize that Asperger's Syndrome is on the autistic spectrum, then more families will be helped.

*Bobby's mom, Vicki, USA, 2000*

# 20

# Life With My AS Mother

## (The feelings of a child from age three through thirteen)

A little girl, confused and in pain
Her ugly face smiles, but all is in vain.
For even her mother, who must be real wise
Cannot bear to look, at her face and her eyes.
And now she starts talking, and proud as can be
But is told to shut up, she stutters you see.
Not easy to follow, a strange sound the boot
It sure puts a damper, on the little girl's mood.
But though as she is, she will try once more
Oh Mom let me help you, with sweeping the floor.
She only gets scolded, get out of my way
Go play in your bedroom, till dinner do stay.
The girl starts to wonder, I must be real bad
I am even in trouble, when hugging my Dad.
For Mom doesn't want that, it's easy to sense
Why do I keep trying, I must be real dense.

The call comes for dinner, she trembles in fear
And walks down real slowly, removing a tear.
She carefully scans, her mom's pretty face
No anger, no sadness, of emotions no trace.
After lots of confusion, on goes a big light
I must be real different, and not very bright.
Oh dearest poor mother, how sad you must be
Having to parent, a daughter like me.
No wonder you always, depressed and so down
Your face just like stone, with sometimes a frown.
I try so very hard, not to screw up your life
To give my dear Dad, a happy smiling wife.
And so life goes on, for a couple of years
At night in her bed, the girl sheds her tears.
Why do you so hate me, am I really that bad
I am very lonely, feel stupid and sad.
Then it happens, because she turned six
off to grade one, with others she must mix.
With trembling fear, her head hanging down
and fully expecting the teacher will frown.
A soft gentle voice, just did call her name
she must lift her head, and does so in shame.
The teacher just smiles, and says "Oh my dear"
We're all very nice, please do not have fear.
And nobody laughs, from repulsion no trace
Can they really not see, her sad ugly face?
She's told she is nice, very pretty and smart
She finally does find some joy in her heart
She really loves school, and does start to bloom
She is living a life between joy and real gloom.

Now harder then ever, for mom she is reaching
The only reward, blank stares and some preaching.
Her face is scrunched up, her body goes wild
The total frustration of a stuttering child.
They call her mean names, they laugh and they
    mimic
As if it was funny, some wonderful gimmick
She runs in the house, crying and shaking
But mom has no time, for supper she is making.
From the kitchen she yells, I am sorry my dear
Now please settle down, you are hurting my ear.
With high grades to show, she walks in the door
It is a real shock, to see mom on the floor.
Big brother says quiet, no she is not dead
please get me a blanket, a pillow for her head.
Your news must be good, it just cannot miss
You better get used to this, dear little sis.
Her eyes say the words, I don't understand
He just pats her hair, then lets go of her hand.
And so it continues, year in and year out
She becomes very quiet, her brother real loud.
While he gets attention, she just fades away
No longer she speaks, nor join kids for some play
Gymnastics she joins, it's just down the street
You don't have to bring me, I will be real sweet.
I love it, oh Mom this really is life
I am doing real good, for perfection I strive.
A city wide contest, to show off your skill
Dear Mom please come watch me, say that you will.
I know I won't win, with my figure all wrong

But having you there, will make me feel strong.
With tears in her heart, a smile on her face
She concentrates hard, it is a close race.
While all join the party, in a corner she stands
So sad and alone, clutching the gold in her hands.
Her girl in the spotlight, mom's greatest fear
So tears and depression, conveniently appear.
Mom it's so obvious, it's always the same
I silently call it, your suicide game.
While carefully planning the day she will die
She feels so at peace, she doesn't know why.
He came out of nowhere, this caring young man
his unexplained presence, screwed up her plan.
It is not your time yet, the message was clear
You will find your path, it's inside you my dear.
But years of true love, has not found the key
To unlock the doors, to free the real me.

*Paula, Canada, 2002*

## 21

# Disconnecting from the Treadmill

I met my, as yet undiagnosed, AS husband, E, at a time when I was emotionally very needy. I was a single mom, raising a little boy. My first marriage had failed, and I thanked my lucky stars that I had full custody of my son. His father completely ignored him, and we didn't have to contend with rival custody issues.

I was eagerly looking forward to meeting someone special, and along came E.

On the surface he seemed very pleasant. He was very free with the compliments and had an accommodating personality. I really admired his mind – brilliant! There wasn't a single topic that he was unfamiliar with. Plus, he had custody of his three children, from his previous marriage! As far as I was concerned, that spoke volumes about his personality and priorities. He had a pretty decent job (systems analyst), he was head-over-heels in love with me, and he got on really well with my son. His kids were amenable to the relationship, and we made ourselves into a family.

Happily ever after? No! Mind you, this is not about AS bashing. This is an "awareness" guide, a chronicle of insidious behavior and presentation, that will serve to either alert, or validate. In my case, the symptoms crept up very slowly and relentlessly, for a period of twenty-two years, before they reached a crescendo.

It all began with issues of control. He needed to control all aspects of our family life. He decided on the level of "religious" practice, and would follow everyone around (including me) to make sure that we were conforming to his requirements. When I would complain that this was humiliating to me, he would say that it was his duty as head of the house, to "keep an eye on us!" I was raised in a genuinely religious home, and something like his lack of trust was glaring me in the face!

This hooked into control of all money matters. I would beg him to just give me a specific, agreed-upon sum of money, and I would budget the household expenses. Now, I have to admit, I was pretty good at this. My mother (may she rest in peace) gave me a very thorough course in budgeting (which she learned first-hand, as a Holocaust survivor). He, on the other hand, came to the marriage with a $15,000 debt!! I tried to explain, in a very nice way, that I believed I had better experience with finances. I was told to "stay by the frying pan," while he managed our affairs!

He had a hyper-developed sense of humor that he called upon constantly to rescue him from uncomfortable situations. So the control issues were usually blanketed with a helping of "humor." As the years wore on, the humor was refined to caustic puns. These puns were directed at me, couched in humor, me being the butt of the joke, of course.

They were so sheathed, and so direct, that anyone sitting around the table would not catch it, and if I responded, he would jump right in, and declare how "sensitive" I was.

We did very little entertaining, and practically never went out together. He would say that he found me so special that it was enough for him to just sit with me by the fireside (we don't have a working one) and enjoy my presence. By this time, we had seven children (other than the step-sibs), and I wouldn't have minded going out and being treated like a woman instead of a breeder. Although I love and adore each of my kids, I couldn't escape the fact that something very big was missing from my life. But I couldn't put my finger on it...yet.

As time wore on, and the family became bigger, more demands were made on him. His paycheck was pitifully insufficient. He tried tutoring, but made pennies when we needed bucks. He wrote stories on the side that took him forever to complete. He was never up for promotion at work, because he was hopelessly irregular with his time sheet. It didn't make sense. Here was a brilliant man who just couldn't get it done. But, more importantly, he didn't think there was a problem!

With ten kids to feed, I took matters into my own hands, and opened a fashion jewelry retail store. I got an investor to help with renovations and operated out of my former garage! Needless to say, our relationship really slipped. He couldn't handle the fact that he had no say, or control over the business, it's income, or the spending of the proceeds. He never lost an opportunity to downgrade my efforts, the time spent in my store, or to loudly exclaim that since he never really saw the hard cash, maybe the whole endeavor just wasn't worth it!

Ten years into our marriage, my mother passed away. She had been ill for a number of years, and I remember running back and forth between our houses to help out. At the time I thought that E seemed emotionally detached from the million crises that would erupt, but I thought that it was out of respect for my mother (read "female") that he never really got involved. He would mechanically "fill in" when asked to do something, but he never showed any emotion.

When it came to emotions, the only word to describe them would be "wooden." His emotions were expressed by rote, as though he was taught to respond that way. I got the sense that he was "faking" it. He didn't come through as sincere. He also exhibited a strange lack of empathy.

Here's where the doubts really began to set in. What did lack of empathy mean to me? It meant my AS husband falling asleep in a chair, as I was laboring in pain during childbirth. It meant coming home after my mother's funeral, and not having an empathetic husband to turn to in such a time of severe grief. It meant my daughter writhing in pain during a kidney stone attack, and he wouldn't let me into the locked bathroom before I (not he) got her to the hospital. It meant crying into my pillow at night, in deep anguish, while he snored like a beached whale!

Then there was the issue of remorse – or lack of! No matter what went wrong, it was never his fault. It was always my fault. Everything was my fault. Whatever secret situation (and everything was always a secret) was bothering him, it was my fault. I had to be able to read his mind, solve his problems, and if I couldn't then I was a failure. Now for the life of me, I had no clue as to what was bothering him. I had to read his mind, yet he couldn't read mine, or his *own*! He had no clue what was in my mind or in my heart. He didn't know me or himself. That's known as *mind blind*!

He had no clue how his actions or inactions impacted on those around him, namely his wife and family. I once asked him if he knew what part he played in the destruction of our marriage, or if he thought that he should apologize in any way, and he answered: "To the degree that you think it's my fault, I apologize!" Brilliant. That statement summed it up for me.

My running on the treadmill of my marriage came to a halt when he jeopardized the family in a criminal and irresponsible way. I warned him that if he would continue in this manner, he should not bother coming home, and I would lock him out. He called my bluff, and the rest is history!

It's been a year now, and he's really out for good. He remains undiagnosed, but at least I have the security that the kids and myself will no longer be subject to his AS parenting and "spousing." The kids have suffered terribly. He was not a dad to them. He was mostly "out to lunch." They love him, but he's not "in their face," and, from a distance, tolerable. I'm presently trying to negotiate a divorce, but he's not co-operating. He won't let me "break up the family."

In all this time, the words "I'm sorry" have never crossed his lips, nor have the words "I love you and want to make this work." Twenty-two years of unreturned love and sacrifice have gone by and, thankfully, I've stepped off the treadmill. I'm on my own now, but then again, I've always been alone. Now it's time for self-respect, dignity, and the ability to believe in improvements and progress.

*Regina, New York, 2001*

## 22

# When Love is Not Enough

I thought that I could write a book about what it was like living with a husband who has Asperger's Syndrome, although you don't know at the time that is what it is. It is like a dripping tap that eventually erodes enamel, the grinding down of your self-esteem, self-confidence, morale, sense of humor, even sanity – it becomes like living in a nightmare from which you never wake up, you wonder if you are going mad or if you are the only sane one in a mad world. The toll on your health can manifest as physical illness or depression or both. I have pages and pages of scribblings and notes; it is supposed to be helpful to write your feelings down. I certainly would have enough material to write a book, but everybody who is in the same situation could write a book, so I will try to restrict myself to the things which caused me to think that there was something incomprehensible the matter, that it was something to do with perception, cognition and comprehension, and the things which would be most helpful for somebody in the same situation to know about.

Behavior that baffles, bewilders and confuses you, and is sometimes bizarre. Continual misunderstandings and misinterpretations that cause confusion, chaos, havoc, anxiety and anger. Why did he do that? Why did he say that? Why didn't he do that? Why didn't he say that? Behavior that contradicts what he said or did before, or thinks other people should or should not do.

One of the most baffling things was the lack of perception about other people's intentions, or why somebody would or would not want to do something. All the unwritten rules of behavior were puzzling to him. Concepts about what is considered "normal" were puzzling. Something which you think is obvious is not to him. Something which you think is self-explanatory is not to him. Apparent gross selfishness and self-centered behavior; he would often get his own way because he did not recognize the needs of others. He will not listen to explanations; he just wants "the bottom line".

You talk about something or mention something and you think he is going to do something that he doesn't do, he expresses surprise that you are cross he hasn't done it. You do something and he says he didn't know you were going to do it, but you had told him. He cannot "discuss" things in the sense of talking "about" something, weighing up the pros and cons, looking at it from several different angles to decide on the best course of action, looking at the consequences or knock-on effect; he just agrees with the first thing you say.

You talk about something using the same words, but it turns out he has a different understanding of the meaning of some words to what your understanding is. You argue for twenty minutes bafflingly and it turns out, when you eventually manage to analyze what it is he is saying, that he agrees with you.

Why does he do things that appear to be stupid? Is he stupid? How can he be stupid when he can do things he wouldn't be able to do if he was stupid? A lot of misunderstandings about meeting in a certain place or at a certain time. Whenever he does not do what you thought he was going to do and you ask for an explanation, his explanation baffles you even more and raises a dozen more questions.

He cannot work out bus or train timetables based on a twenty-four-hour clock or work the central heating time clock. He cannot play "Chopsticks" on the piano even when he is shown very slowly and shown it is just repeating the same thing.

Whenever he does something like DIY it is as though it is the first time he has done it. He does not seem to learn from his experiences or have a memory bank of past experiences. He looks at a job that needs doing and says, oh, it's just this and that. After he has started he gets into all kinds of difficulties and mess but insists on carrying on even when things are obviously getting worse and worse.

He insists on doing things that you would much rather he did not do but left to somebody who knows. It is not a disgrace if you don't know how to do plumbing or carpentry or electrics; they are jobs people spend years learning. I grew to panic if I saw him with a screwdriver or oil can in his hand.

He once destroyed every electrical appliance in the house by plugging them into a socket that blew the fuse, and would not be told that it must be something the matter with the socket. He once cut through the wire of an alarm bell in a shop and the alarm set off and it took me half an hour to find an electrician to come and stop it.

If he was fitting carpets, the carpet – which had originally been bigger than the room so it could be fitted in one piece – ended up like a jigsaw puzzle with little pieces fitting in all round the corners and central heating pipes, which came up in the Hoover. It was like being married to a cross between Peter Pan and Frank Spencer.

The first time I left him with our new baby aged three weeks, I put the sleeping baby into his arms in the car whilst I went to find somebody. I was away fifteen minutes and when I got back the baby was screaming and he was holding him in exactly the same position as when I had left him and was cross because ladies had been looking in the window of the car to see what was the matter. I had to put our babies into his arms or he would never have picked them up and cuddled them.

It was as if to him the interest he had in our children was like my interest in a neighbour's children would be. He never showed tenderness; if they fell over it was, "Oh, get up you're all right." In a domestic crisis he was hopeless and helpless. He had some holiday owing when I was seven months' pregnant with our second child. I wanted to go somewhere not too far away from our home in the northwest of England. We went to the Isle of Wight! He had not realized you had to book a ferry place and we had a five-hour wait in the queue. When our turn came to drive onto the ship he was missing in the toilets. We had no accommodation booked ("Oh, we'll get something when we arrive"), and he said he felt like Joseph going round the hotels trying to find us a room late in the evening.

The first time we moved house, we hired a van, and his father and brother helped us to move. I reminded him several times about the garage needing emptying. When they had finished and taken the van back I realized that the items from the garage were missing. "Oh, there wasn't time, just leave them, it doesn't matter." He refused to go back (only a mile away) to collect the things from the garage.

He had a week off work to help us get settled in, but behaved as though he was on holiday. He could not see what needed to be done and when the central heating didn't work, etc. refused to go to see the Site Engineer to complain. I thought the hot water tank was going to explode in the night; the thermostat had not been fitted, and he just lay there while I sprang out of bed to see what was the matter and turn on the hot water to relieve the banging and turn off the immersion.

Once, when we had a shop, I heard breaking glass in the middle of the night and woke him up. "Oh, it's probably just a milk bottle", he said. I went down and the shop window was broken; we had to phone up the emergency glass fitters. His watch broke and he borrowed mine. He left it in the pocket of his work overalls that get sent to the laundry, and then laughed when he realized what had happened. He did not apologize or replace my watch or realize that I missed it. Indeed I wondered if he had a conscience; he never seemed to feel remorse, express regret, kick himself or wish he had done something differently. He said it was no use crying over spilt milk. He did not seem to be able to project his mind into a hypothetical situation to work out what you would do then, or put himself in somebody else's shoes to see what it would feel like.

He does not seem to "miss" people or feel a sense of loss or yearning, but if you asked him if he was close to his family he would say yes. When his father died he made jokes at the funeral because everybody was too solemn. After the King's Cross fire and Zeebrugge ferry disasters he said there would be more jobs available for more people. When we were watching the news he would make comments which not only showed a lack of sympathy or empathy but also showed he had missed the meaning of what was being said.

When our son was six and broke his arm at school in the morning, I spent all day at the hospital with him and our daughter aged three. I phoned my husband's work to tell him what had happened and he came to the hospital when he had finished work in the late afternoon. When our son was fourteen he broke his leg and for months was encased in plaster from toe to hip. I helped him into the bath daily and propped his leg up so it wouldn't get wet and used the shower attachment to help him to bathe. When I suggested to my husband that it would be a good thing if he could help to do this he refused.

I always had to organize everything, plan everything, suggest what he should do to help, deal with all the business side, mortgage, insurance, etc. He did not seem to have any initiative. If I asked him to take over a job because I had so much to do, it turned out wrong.

If we went out in the evening and he was in the company of his family and their friends, people he had known a long time, he was like a person in an audition for *The Comedians*, laughing, dancing, joking, very extrovert, drinking, he was usually sick on the way home. If he did not know the company he went to the other extreme and sat in silence, looking like a hunted animal, never making any attempt to socialize or be agreeable. He did not like the husbands of any of my friends so we never visited them, and he made remarks which ridiculed members of my family, until I fell out with one of them, when he bent over backwards to be nice to them.

He decided to give up smoking when he was about sixteen and that was it – he never had another cigarette and did not seem to have withdrawal symptoms or cravings. He says it is just willpower. If he puts on too much weight and decides to go on a diet he just gives up food. When he decided to cut me out of his life it was as though we had never been a partnership and had never meant anything to each other.

When we first had a shop and a customer complained about a mistake that had been made, he just stood and looked at the custumer. After I had told him he should apologize to the customer and put things right, he did so.

If the children tried to cuddle him, he used to say "you're potty" or "put me down, you don't know where I've been". I never saw him cry. He said he did cry when he went to see *Born Free*. He never asked questions or showed curiosity.

A man who worked with him for three years said in all that time he had never mentioned his wife and children. He was a good employee, never late, never ill, always cheerful, always willing. He seemed to escape to work if there were problems at home. "I've got to go to work" was his answer.

Since we split up he has not called me anything – to use my name seems to cause him enormous problems. When I said this to him he disagreed and said it was me. Since we split up he contradicts everything I say, opposes everything I say. He does recognize my material needs but has no perception of my emotional needs or anybody else's emotional needs. He does not seem to have any emotional needs himself. He does not seem to be connected to memories that have involved emotion or feeling.

When we had the confirmation of Asperger's Syndrome, he said if you took a new car to a mechanic he would find fault with it. He absolutely falls into the "extraordinarily tolerant" category, cannot accept the diagnosis, says he is fine as he is, very happy as he is, and cannot see why anybody should have a problem relating to him; if they do then it is their problem. He cannot see that it should make children unhappy and distressed because their parents have split up. He cannot see that his children should be distressed because he does not visit them for weeks when he has ample opportunity to do so. He signed their birthday cards with his name until told they would prefer him to put "Dad".

I could go on and on, but hope this is enough to help others recognise similar symptoms in their own partners.

*Brenda Wall, UK, 1997*

**Update, June 2002**

I found out about Asperger's syndrome from watching a TV programme in December 1995, and we had the diagnosis in June 1996, 10 years after we had split up. Those 10 years were for me a lonely nightmare of emotional trauma, financial worry, family turmoil, depression and melancholy. Family and friends could not believe such a nice man behaved as he did, there were comments such as "six of one and half a dozen of the other" and "hearing the other side". Relate counselling was futile, and none of the psychology books I studied gave an explanation for his behaviour.

Once I knew what the problem was, I set out to learn as much as I could about it and find help for myself to overcome the trauma I had been through. There was no help available in any way shape or form, indeed my doctor did not see why I needed any help, so I started to contact other women with Asperger husbands. We managed to initiate some literature, and from media publicity it was realised that there were thousands of families like ours with Asperger's syndrome in several generations.

Meeting other women who had often suffered more than I had with a husband further down the spectrum, and talking about shared experiences, validated my own feelings and was a source of great relief, comfort and new friendships. Reading everything I could lay my hands on, particularly books written by adults with Aspergers, gave me an understanding of the condition and some insight into what it must be like to suffer from it. The interest of Dr Tony Attwood gave official recognition to our cause, his Workshops for Partners and the wonderful FAAAS mailing list lead to meetings with more marvellous people whose love and understanding has helped me to heal.

I now realise that the Asperger spectrum is huge, and compared to some others my ex-husband is only mildly affected, though I also know many who are less affected than he. I am now able to understand why he behaves as he does, see where his "blind spots" are and know what situations he is likely to find difficult. He still does not accept the diagnosis and I have stopped trying to explain sight to a blind man, he does not want to know and is convinced it is me who is blind.

We are now able to be friends and visits are enjoyed as long as they are short. I know he is basically a kind and generous person who wants to help and has good intentions. His DIY skills have improved and so have his planning and organizing skills. He still exasperates me when he thinks he knows the best way to get from A to B, a distance of 1 mile, and he takes 5 miles to do so. He still misunderstands intention, takes meaning literally, doesn't tell me something but expects me to know, finds others a puzzle and is always criticising them, cannot stand criticism himself and his eyes dart when he is under pressure. I still love him but I know we shall never get back together, and I will never love anybody else – I have learned to live with it.

*23*

# My Corner

I am a good girl.
I sit still and behave myself.
I try harder than possible.

Still my feet are kicked.
I tuck them tightly under my chair.

And they are kicked.
Sometimes it pains.
Sometimes it's just to be reminded.

I stretch them out.
And they are kicked.
That sears all the way to my breast.

I hide them again and I think of my space.
They are so far back, only the toes touch the floor.
And they get kicked.
The consistency is both enraging and easy to ignore.

My tantrum rocks the house. Surprise.
Everyone holds on, peeking out, until it subsides.

I want to be a good girl.
I will sit on my chair and behave myself.

And my feet are kicked.

I sit in my chair and
hide my face.
(someone might notice)

It comes from deep within. Far down.
(I take the elevator down to look)

It regurgitates up.
Waves and
Waves of it.

I cough it into my hands.
I look down the shaft and see me.

I see me folding in half.
another wave.
I fold in half again.
another wave.
In half again.
Nine times.
I get smaller each time.
Until I am a pinpoint of light.

The light does not go away.
It is surrounded by darkness
and silence.

What's behind the door?
Dark or light
Loss or hope
I cannot bear to look,
My arms are too weak to try.

I can't reach
I can't move
I sit on my chair
with my feet tucked tightly underneath
and I hide my face.

*Yvette Gerhardt, USA, 2003*

*24*

# My Older AS Son...

My older son with AS was an unusual baby – something I realized even more in hindsight than when nurturing him.

At the time I was amazed at how very little sleep he needed, how he fought sleep, wriggled with discomfort at being cuddled, until he was always held looking outwards, never in a cradle hold, and seemed hyperactive. He was exhausting without being rewarding the way the other babies were – unloving, pushed away from kisses and wiped away the few that landed.

People never warmed to him, except his eccentric grandfather. I was intrigued to find I could set my watch to his waking for a feed – as routine as a bottle-fed infant, but not keen at all in long-term and baby-led weaning like the siblings.

He became a real loner. Loving books more than people, passed milestones incredibly fast. Being exhausting to keep up with, communication was about information as he got older, never about his inner thoughts or feelings. Now at twenty-six three relationships have broken due to this.

He was looked on as disruptive at school, especially when changing levels or schools. I spent hours advocating for him (now wish I'd practised tough love to instill social mores stronger than I did – the way Victorian parents helped my husband who now gets along with outsiders, especially older people) when I thought he was not extended, and therefore bored, because he is so bright. Absorbing facts effortlessly – he memorized the underground in London within days, aged twelve years, when we visited the UK from a developing country without even exposure to motorways!

I would say that he uses pot/marijuana to self-medicate, trying to fit in, be more like others. Teachers called him cussed, and he has lost a job due to staff petitioning against his "arrogant" ways with staff and clients, though fifty per cent find find him charming and informative – as long as they don't challenge his phenomenal knowledge.

He has really estranged his younger brother, seeming callous, superior and arrogant, yet it's so unlike his siblings, who have not modeled on that from their father (who is almost excruciatingly mannerly; though it made me feel special when we dated, and certainly entraps other women, often intellectual, not feeling ones – the wide blue-eyed gaze!).

His relationship with his sister is not as an equal, and somewhat teasing, distant, though not too uncomfortable. She is assertive in a healthier way than I ever could be with my husband, who is intolerant of children's normal behavior. I was demoralized by my husband's manner, without realizing it, and suffered massive loss of self-esteem – I have a science degree and teaching qualification, but feel incapable of using them.

My husband had unhappy school years and repeated a failed final year, and then once into tertiary study, he spent thirteen years there full time. Not knowing what to do with life, until medicine became an absorption after years in chemistry. In the early years with him, he was frequently depressed and I would feel it was my fault. I spent hours reading relationship books, wondering what was wrong with *me* – though I am actually very perceptive and accepting in relationships.

I miscarried at home when midterm, and he did not want to see the infant, or let the boys, and had me flush it down the loo – this from a GP...no discussion. And whenever I or the children had health issues or operations, he was either not there for us, or would be clinically interested, never empathetic, though patients find him caring, charming and communicative. We in the family find he cannot be affirmative, affectionate, accepting or acknowledging. I used to long for him to agree with me on anything! His daughter used to cry when her friends had him as GP and said she was lucky to have such a nice father.

Now, sure, the plumber's pipes may leak, but this was in a different dimension – he cannot operate in a close emotional family relationship. When he tries to, we find the "rote" phrases used on patients wear thin. He answers their phone calls with "not a problem" at any time of day, yet we have to drag a sentence out at a time – often over several days.

Obsessive compulsive about work, he is maniacal about time. Adhering rigidly to routines, and surviving in general practice due to the comfort of bookings/schedules/the routine. Being master of the moment. Good diagnostically, but known as the stress doctor because he always goes into a routine about that, regardless – though of course it often applies! His patients never have to wait due to his fetish – just as well he doesn't deliver babies. Patients find him charming (especially to older people), communicative and caring (the rote-learned question to carers and mothers, "And how are you in all this?" really impresses them).

But it's not like that in the family, where we need acknowledgement, acceptance, appreciation and affection.

*Anonymous, New Zealand, 2002*

# 25

# Tempest and Sunshine

Brave, with the lights on
Perpetual drama on a private stage,
Rock star, Rambo, Intergalactic hero,
Mighty ships sink in tumultuous seas
And heroes don't do battle with the wind.
So, store your heavy artillery,
Calm your fair weather storms,
Let the breezes blow more gently
And share the magic of your quiet dreams,
Your happy building dreams,
With Me.

*Cynthia Marchant, USA, 1990*

*26*

# AS Awareness: A Path Out of the Darkness

As a teacher, I had known the term Asperger's Syndrome for several years. It was one of many disorders associated with my daughter's special needs classmates. But recently one of my own students displayed behaviors similar to my daughter's and those of her friends. I needed information on teaching this young boy who, like my daughter, did not have an official diagnosis. He was not even in a special class, but he was very different and needed to be taught differently; that I knew.

The Internet was my constant source of information. Through efforts to develop teaching strategies, I soon began to find names and descriptions of childhood disorders that matched his characteristics. As I located the Autism Spectrum, it was obvious that not only my student, but also my daughter, fell within this category. She did not fit neatly into one of the particular disorders listed, but a label existed for that! PDD-NOS: Pervasive Developmental Disorder – Not Otherwise Specified. I was not, at that time, as interested in a diagnosis as I was with understanding the autism spectrum in general.

When I began to read more about Asperger's Syndrome as a high functioning form of autism, I knew I'd found my student's niche. He was definitely a "Little Professor." The introductory material described him to a tee. So I read on and on. What I discovered brought tears to my eyes and a huge weight was lifted from my soul. I was reading about people who lacked an ability to understand the feelings, the needs, and practically the existence of other people. They could be intelligent, gentle, loyal and honest. They were focused individuals who understood their own needs and pursued their interests vigorously. But they were impaired in their ability to develop appropriate social relationships with others. I was reading about my *husband*. His obsessions with astronomy and physics, his rigidity with meals and schedules, his difficulty in accepting change, his resistance to loving touches, and his inability to share in my interests.

My husband is a university professor, focused in his areas of expertise, yet completely oblivious to the need for skills in any other areas, especially social. Our relationship began and was developed based on my sharing of his interests. What I mistook for caring, early on, was in fact his obsession for me. When we were first married with no children, my life was whatever *he* wanted or *he* needed and I derived my satisfaction from that. This man was clearly centered. He knew what he wanted and where he was going. It was a strength of character that I admired. I was no wimp myself, and wanted to marry an emotionally secure and dependable type. He was extremely intelligent and seemed pleased that I was also relatively bright. I often questioned the one-sided relationship, but was met with indignation. What did I have to complain about? And everyone, not just my husband, agreed. Look at all the wonderful things we did together, the material goods we had and the bright future ahead. As long as it was just the two of us, I accepted far more of the difficulties than I should have. We put off starting a family so that "we" could do and have the things "we" wanted.

The responsibilities within the marriage were heavily split with little or no overlap. What my husband was good at doing was all he could do. It was the classic, "He can master the theories of nuclear physics, but he can't screw in a light bulb." Financial issues were his main concern. The basic skills for everyday living and loving were left for me to learn alone. I was good at that and a vicious cycle began. Since I was better at doing just about everything, it all became my responsibility. Nothing was accomplished unless I initiated it and that includes our intimate life as well. There were no reciprocating actions, no assistance with chores, no unsolicited compliments or loving attention. Although there was an intense interest in intimate activities, my husband was only capable of receiving and very little giving. His pleasures were based in a fantasy world and not in the reality of a true personal relationship.

Looking in from the outside, it appeared to be a solid marriage. We were active together, doing well financially and well suited for each other. The relationship wasn't really unbearable; it was just frustrating, at first. There was the need to follow routines and to eat certain foods as he always had. There was the lack of need for social interaction even with families. I was happy to oblige him in his thrifty ways, knowing that eventually as we saved together I would be able to spend reasonably as needed. None of these quirks are necessarily unusual, but his response to even a minor discrepancy in any situation was what left a lasting effect. The obvious inability to move on if something did not go his way, the dazed look if I questioned his motive for some irrational act, and the ability to rationalize even the most unusual habit placed him beyond the "men behaving badly" syndrome. Several of his insignificant rituals became seriously compulsive, yet each was rationalized extensively. Most destructive was his inability to recognize my needs even if they were stated clearly to him. "I don't like it when you put the wet towel on my side of the bed," I'd say. And he would respond, "Well, then, you could move it," as that was the obvious thing to do. But six years and many wet towels later, I would cry, "You continue to do this and it hurts my feelings." "No it doesn't" he'd remark, as he'd casually turn and walked away. His reply would drive a wedge between us. But his confused look made it clear he did not understand. I'd ask him if he knew that these were not normal behaviors. Wrong. I told him that I wouldn't mind him being this way if he could just admit that this was unusual. Wrong, again. Always wrong. Always complaining. It was obvious that there was nothing wrong with this marriage, except me and my demands.

There must have been something wrong with me to think that I could ask for more. Was it possible that a loving, fulfilled marriage was really just a myth after all? Could wanting to feel cared about, loved, or understood be unrealistic? I rode a roller-coaster ride of giving and giving, enjoying the ride and waiting for something in return. When we reached the peak and I felt very used, the "complaining" started and down the tubes we went. It was clearly all my fault, yet I knew it wasn't. But it was very confusing. No one seemed to understand what I was talking about, least of all my husband who was blind to the emotions involved. No one else could see the neglect that I felt. My husband refused to discuss our problems and I needed to figure out what was going on. All of the standard efforts to improve relationships seemed to create even more division. Making my needs known became just more complaints in his mind. Reducing my responsibilities became lack of effort. Refusing to participate in his interests without reciprocal actions was termed: Playing Games.

There were generally two responses to my attempts to seek help: 1. he is a fine man, why not take the bad with the good and stop complaining; or 2. he's really a jerk, why don't you just leave him? The first was consistently given by those who knew him and the second by those who were forced to hear my complaints but did not really know him. The dilemma was still there. At times I knew the marriage was different, but special. At other times, I knew I should have left long ago. I was determined to make the marriage work as we began our family.

Not long after the birth of my children and the loving distractions that brought, I allowed the relationship to deteriorate. I had better things to worry about, particularly the care of my daughter, with her unusual needs. My husband was kind and supportive of the children, but accepted no responsibility for their care, or mine. We must all be responsible for our own happiness, you know. I've heard it a million times. There were two possible paths to personal satisfaction in this situation. If I joined my husband in his interests, and accommodated his needs and wishes, we could "all" be happy. Or I could accommodate my needs, following my own road to happiness, only to compromise the security of everyone else. I thought that I could make the paths converge, but found they eventually led into a deep dark cavern instead.

For years, issues that would normally cause us conflict were avoided. Division of financial responsibilities was a classic problem. My husband's obsession with numbers and especially money issues left him capable of quoting all financial accounts to the dime at any given moment. Although I'm sure that we were well within a normal budget, any spending which was not to his personal benefit annoyed him. Using "his" money to pay for my personal needs and interests, including family contacts, always created conflict. Since I offered little financial assistance to the family, I willingly denied myself most of those pleasures. I was quite proud of my thrifty nature including coupon clipping, thrift shop bargains, hand-me-downs, few long-distance phone calls, and practically no visits to be with my family. When the children were old enough I began teaching again, to support the "extras" like clothing, camps, and music lessons. My husband paid for our lovely home, vacations to the places that interested him and, very begrudgingly, for the groceries. Eventually I was able to make trips to visit family, but he had no desire to accompany me. Some of his vacations no longer included me as well. Our finances were his personal business and he would not discuss or share that information with me. I was careful to keep my earnings separate in order to have some discretionary money. He continued to request that I help pay for the groceries. His only other complaint was that he had to pay the taxes on my salary.

Teaching part time and caring for the home and children also kept me too busy to be constantly thinking about our marital problems. This was my husband's reassurance that the problems really were all in my head. Discussions of our disintegrating relationship were eliminated, as were most all conversations unrelated to mutual interests. There was no socializing with peers. He established no friendships and had no interest in mine. As we grew further apart emotionally, intimacy was completely eliminated from the marriage. The children knew that their parents loved them, but not each other. Other than that, they would have everything they needed.

We kept the marriage together. Was it worth it? Were the children really better off? Was it possible to get past the emotional longing and eventually lead a fulfilling life? Why did I still think about it so much? Why did it still seem so confusing? What was it that made me know that this was not just a Mars/Venus issue?

The answer was there in black and white: Asperger's Syndrome, a form of autism, with its apparent genetic links and a possible explanation for our daughter's problems. I studied the subject until I could no longer resist sharing the information. With a small packet of materials covering the basics and printed off the computer, I prepared this letter and presented it to him.

Thursday November 26, 1998

Dear George,

Sorry to be so formal, but we don't seem to be able to communicate on a verbal basis any longer.

Years ago I told you that I did not want to live together in the relationship we had developed. You resisted, not willing to leave, yet refusing to work toward improving the relationship, and I decided that it would be better for the kids if we stuck it out. At that time (a very angry time for me) I was still hoping there would be changes. I vowed to see improvement in the relationship or to get out when the time was right. Obviously, there was no improvement, but at least I have accepted that it will never change and am not so angry anymore. However, the time has come to re-evaluate the ability to live together any longer. Once the kids are gone or on their own, do I want to live like this? Not really. I've told you before that money and material goods would not sway me (though you don't believe that). So, why even ponder the situation? Why not just prepare to leave? Because I don't hate you. I care about you and know that you would not do well on your own (at least not at first!). I dread hurting you too much, but I have to protect myself as well. A mother's job of taking care of everybody else is only workable because there is an end in sight. With you there is no end to the demands for immediate gratification and concern for your every little want or need.

Some people are amazed at how long I've put up with the situation. Others say I brought it on myself, by catering to you for so long. You personally think I just don't appreciate how much you do for me. I think I have a better sense of "people" and know that we all have our quirks and various needs. I didn't mind "putting up" with you because I knew you had to put up with me. But somehow I always thought that eventually you would try to meet my needs as well. It just seemed that you never knew what they were. Or, worst, decided for yourself what they were, and you were wrong. Any effort I made to let you know what my needs were, was labeled "bitching or nagging."

I did not intend to bring up this whole thing for quite some time, but the strangest thing happened. In searching out the information I needed to deal with a little boy I teach, I found you! I've always known that you were a little different. In fact, I think that's what attracted me to you. Even before we married, there were a few things that made me very nervous. At one point, when I was living in Virginia talking to you almost every night, I almost called off the wedding. But my concerns seemed like such a picky little part of who you were, how could I let it keep me from marrying such a fine person, that I cared very deeply for?

Later, as some of these "little" things began to eat away at our relationship, I remember questioning how normal this was. Shouldn't he be able to see what's going on? Why does he not understand? How can his view be so different than mine? I assumed it was a male/female thing. Or that I was naive to the very different ways that people could actually be. Maybe you were just raised very differently than I? Yet I knew there were an awful lot of people that weren't the way you were! Over the years, I've given it many labels: self-centered, obsessive, controlling, inflexible, uninterested in others, lack of concern for others' needs…you name it. Two things stand out, though. One is that I knew you meant no harm, by being the way you were. You are a good person. Second, I always thought (and said, on many occasions) that if you could just see or understand who you were, I could live with it. Instead of denying that your behaviors were unusual, if you admitted that they were there and sometimes difficult to live with, things would be much different. After all, look how difficult I can be to live with!

Now, in a last-ditch effort to change our relationship (God help me for still trying!) I want you to read the following articles carefully. Don't judge, just read. Don't deny, just think. There is still a slim chance that you will understand where I have been coming from, if and when you understand who you are! I hate to issue an ultimatum, but if you don't get it, I can't see any hope of going on together. So, if you don't get it, then figure out a way to get it. Ask questions, or discuss it with someone. Or get some books and read more. Don't make the mistake of thinking it doesn't matter (as you seem to have for so long). Get your priorities straight, unless you think that living alone suits you (and I don't believe it does). Don't get defensive; my offense is way too strong for any defense you put up right now!

I have always cared very deeply for you. But I've always hated some of the things you do. Your inability to change those things made me feel that you couldn't possibly care about me (though deep down I thought you did). Most people need to feel loved and cared for. In spite of what you may think, you have never been able to demonstrate that to me. In addition, your inability to accept responsibilities for meeting some of my basic needs has taken me away from those people (i.e. family and friends) who are able to demonstrate their love for me.

My organized thoughts are deteriorating into ramblings, so I'll end here. Understand that there is much more to be said and done. It is your choice. If you choose by default and do nothing, it is still your choice. I am really tired of "taking the initiative."

Love ? ? ?,

Debbie

The initial comment on the packet of material defining Asperger's Syndrome was, "This sounds like me." And that was it, for over a year. There was no discussion, no additional reading, no research, but there was what appeared to be an occasional effort to behave as normally expected. Unfortunately, those were futile because, characteristic of Asperger, the ability to read what others expect is impaired.

In the past year, I have found the support of other spouses who are in this same predicament. This has relieved some of the feelings of guilt associated with my role in the deterioration of the marriage. Our discussions have shown me the consistency in thinking patterns within the AS brain and provided me with some coping mechanisms to prevent serious problems from arising. They have helped to make me more aware of why I have done and said things that I have. However, the information has yet to keep me from doing more of the same. Understanding that my husband is hard wired to behave in this manner does not fully protect me from the hurt that it inflicts. If this is a condition like so many other handicaps, am I obliged to accept it as it is? Anyone can be involved in a committed relationship only to find out later that there is an obstacle to overcome. What responsibilities do we each have in that process? Awareness and acceptance of this unique situation has created the path to recovery, but it surely must be walked together, even if one is being led by the other. And that is very slow in coming.

I have continued to look for professional assistance and met with much resistance. Unless my husband is willing to seek out the information himself, there is no one who will attempt to inform him or help him. In addition, lack of information and experience within the medical and mental health professions regarding autistic behaviors creates an uncertain ability to be properly diagnosed and cared for. One psychiatrist that I spoke with, seeking information on the diagnosis process, stated firmly that my husband could not have Asperger's Syndrome because our twenty-five-year marriage negated the requirement of impaired ability to maintain social relationships. However, after one session of describing my husband and our marriage, I believe I had offered this professional far more insight than he was able to offer me. The dilemma continues to exist. If I try to persuade my husband to seek help, I am the complainer, the problem. If I resist the efforts to initiate changes, I'm the one not trying, and if I just ignore it all, everything continues as before.

The recent exposure of Asperger's Syndrome through national publications has afforded me some opportunities to keep my husband informed. There have been a few interactions at home that suggest he is more aware than he lets on. During one major disagreement recently, my daughter accused my husband of initiating the argument with an inappropriate comment to me. He exclaimed, "Heaven forbid that anything I say should upset your mother." It was the first time in twenty-six years of marriage that I had heard him admit that he could have been the source of irritation. Another time, I got my just dues. I asked him why, when requested to help set up for dinner, he had put six different bottles of salad dressing on the table. He responded, "If I had selected just the one I wanted, you would have complained that I only think of myself." And he's right, I would have. He could never have known which dressing I preferred, as he would never have taken notice and he certainly would never have thought to ask. Yet he knew that his first reaction, getting only what he wanted, was not appropriate. This is progress.

There is hope for the future, though maybe not for my marriage. It is hope for the awareness of AS and other autistic disorders which act as a hidden handicap. When the general public, the medical profession, and those living with these circumstances have a better understanding of the neurological differences between people, a brighter light will shine for everyone.

*Debbie, USA, 2000*

# 27

# Passive Aggression

The term "passive aggression"
Seems to be an anomaly.
Not making sense.
Ridiculous,
Absurd,
Words that are contradictory.

Passive, inert, and submissive –
Showing lack of excitement.
Making no effort.
Ignoring,
Limp
Appearing to be obedient.

Aggression unprovoked attack
The initiation of a quarrel.
To take the offensive.
Violent,
Active,
Perpetrating and forceful.

Passive Aggression is unprovoked attack
By ignoring the needs of others.
Walking away,
Denying,
Smiling while another suffers.


*Passive Aggression* © *Copyright 2002 Marguerite Long*

Email author marguerite@rosesandcacti.com

The author grants permission to copy this document provided it is for non-commercial purposes, is complete, unaltered and retains this copyright message.

## 28

# Six Generations of AS

Asperger's Syndrome, as I have perceived and experienced it, runs through six generations of my wife's family, from her grandfather to a fully autistic great-granddaughter. After experiencing it for the last difficult, frustrating, and confusing fifty-four years, I look at the syndrome's effect as somewhat of a trilogy of the extended family, the AS person, and the immediate family care-giver. It often includes various members of the family's generations and, in turn, almost always affects the entire family to different degrees. It also affects the primary family member who has AS (spouse in my case) according to the degree of AS severity. And it perhaps most directly affects the family care-giver, both by how severe the family member suffers from AS and, perhaps most importantly, how successfully the care-giver can adjust to the behavior of the AS person.

It has been my experience that AS sufferers have qualities which could be rated as "plus" factors (i.e. Einstein memories, etc.), and others which could be called "minus" factors (controllers, insensitivity, etc.). I have seen them, on a moment-to-moment basis, display the plus behaviors to the public and decidedly minus behaviors to their inner circle of family. It is often the "mix and match" quality of the syndrome which makes them attractive to the world and at the same time intolerable to their family and/or mates. I often have visualized my AS family members as having a circular target of rings (like a bow and arrow target). The care-giver(s) was the bull's-eye and got all of the minus factors while the rest of the family/world as outer rings were given only the plus factors. I will continue to use the parochial terms of plus and minus in the following and will mention only a few AS characteristics.

My wife's grandfather was described as "had a real good memory but was shy," making him still in the plus area generally. Her mother had a superior memory and engaging personality, but treated everyone alike (only one level of sensitivity), tended to be "a homebody" but is still a high plus person. My wife has a superior memory and a plus personality with public and family, but is a controller, lacks genuine affection (I have chosen celibacy for over thirty years rather than deal with intimacy otherwise) and is shrewdly manipulative and selectively honest. Consequently, she is a public and family plus, while being a high minus with her inner circle of me. In my opinion, if I hadn't adjusted, she would have had a much more difficult life. My oldest son has all of his mother's behaviors but to a greater degree. And he has added a few minuses like a lack of common sense. He's suffered professionally, his wife divorced him, his children have little love for him and he's been on the verge of suicide several times. His oldest daughter was diagnosed with AS in her earlier twenties. Both parents have never acknowledged her disability thereby denying her much needed help. She is unable to live as an independent adult and exhibits: no sense of virtue, always repeats things, has little-to-none sensitivity and/or gratitude and a strong need for strict order in her life. She has had two children out of wedlock, the first of which has been diagnosed as a severely autistic child.

There are others in my family (male and female siblings) whom I also suspect have a degree of AS in their make-up but, in the interest of time, this family description will have to suffice. However, it does bring up a few questions. How much is AS "selectively" inherited? Does it affect the first child more than others? Do AS people have a "two-faced" personality more than normal people? Does AS get more serious as it is passed on? Is it a recessive gene in those children of an AS parent who are apparently normal which will eventually surface in one of their children? So, as we all know, there is plenty that we don't know.

However, I've been blessed to know the following: I have a firm testimony that the most help I can get is that I receive from Heavenly Father. I believe that this life is just a test of how consistently we can response with Christlike love to this particular "cross" (and others) in this world. I believe in the eternal nature of the family and that the mortal coat of AS will be removed from my wife in the post-mortal life. The challenge then, if one has decided to remain in the AS relationship, is to "endure it well," and I hope and pray that we all can.

*A seventy-plus-year-young anonymous man, USA*

# 29

# Trying to Describe Our Situation

I have been trying for days to come up with the words that best describe our situation. My son was diagnosed with Asperger's Syndrome a little over two years ago. When did I start to take a good look at my husband? Shortly after the specialist I saw for my son informed me that Asperger's usually shows up on the father's side. I have always known that my husband was a little different. Things such as calling his father "Daddy" when we first started dating I found to be endearing and naive. My husband has always been a little immature for his age. Looking back, maybe I needed someone at that time in my life to look after. He was hopelessly sweet but he also had a temper. He also was a very social person, and that appealed to me because I was too. It was shortly after we were married that I learned that I had been duped. All the socializing had been done with the aid of alcohol, in order to be able to get through the social anxiety. The need to be with me and converse with me was just to get me. Now that he had me he felt he didn't need to talk to me at all that much anymore unless we were discussing something of high interest to him. This has never culminated into a discussion about our relationship. Any discussion about us is warded off with a "later, or not now" or, if cornered, with verbal abuse. Sounds pretty black. But it's not always that bad. I have learned very well how to work within his comfort level. That is the trick to learning to live with someone you love that has AS. If you can get to the point, and believe me it has taken thirteen years of tears and frustration to get there, where you understand that their whole life revolves around taking care of their safety or comfort level, you'll do OK. It allows you to forgive a lot and look past a lot. No, he doesn't hate you and your family, it's just that attending a wedding in a strange place with people he doesn't know mixed in with people he does know is an absolutely, unbelievably scary thing for him to do. He will say and do anything to upset you so that you give up on the idea of going with him. He needs to feel safe and he will do anything to maintain that. It used to be that I felt so hurt. How could he be so self-centered? How could he not care about how I feel? He cares, he just can't feel that out of control of his environment.

If I really want to do something now that includes him, I let him know why I want to do this, why it is very important to me, state why it is the right thing to do, they came to our wedding, etc., and then I don't argue with him. Nine times out of ten he will go. If I push it, it just adds to the anxiety. Yes, he'll try to pick a fight that day as an excuse to get out of it but I have got his number, and I don't bite. Then once we are there he usually calms down enough to enjoy himself. A lot of work, I know, that's why I pick very carefully what I would like him to attend with me. I'm at the point in my life that if others don't understand, I don't care much. Those I am close to understand or at least try to understand what's going on with my husband. They have all had their one-on-one experiences with him and they all like him. My husband does great when there is just him and one or two other people. So if other people get offended with that I don't get upset about it. My husband is who he is. I wish that it was different sometimes and so does he. He has refused to even try any medication. I guess that I will have to respect his choice.

We used to fight horribly. Sometimes we still do, nothing like it used to be. First of all my son is extremely sensitive to loud noises. This has been a great asset to us. It has forced us to tone it down. Second, if he begins to engage in mud-slinging I immediately leave the room. I sit down and try to figure out why this subject is of such discomfort to him. This is extremely hard to do. Sometimes I go for a walk or pack the kids in the car and go for a visit to my Mom's. I don't want my son and daughter exposed to this anymore so if it comes to mudslinging I'm out of there. When an AS person rages he or she goes totally out of control. My son can be the same way. My husband has told me how upset he has been with himself when he gets like this. He says that he wants to stop and it's like the anger has taken a life of its own. That's why a lot of the time I leave. This was learned, yet the hard way. Who did he think he was talking to this way? How dare he break things in my house! If I leave we don't get to this point. He doesn't feel like crap about himself and I can take a breather myself and, like I said before, have a think about why this particular subject is setting off bells in him. I am not always perfect at this. I'm not always great at doing this. Every day I have to remind myself that I am living with an adult and a child with AS. It's not fair, it's not right, it just is. I love them both.

My husband is a good man. He loves me to pieces. I honestly get my way in most issues. He is very affectionate but not a great conversationalist. I long for the talks we had when we were going together. I have to constantly pull him away from the computer to spend time with the family. This has been the most recent bone of contention. Common sense and reason – aspies love logic even when it doesn't go in their favor – usually gets him to see it my way. This time it is taking more time than usual. I will not give up on this one. I think I almost got it worked out. He needs his computer time and we need his family time so he gets his computer from the time he gets home from work at 2:30 p.m. until dinner; after that we get him. He's resisting but sees the fairness in it. He hates it when I point out to him that sometimes things don't have logic; it's just the right thing to do.

I guess I'll end in saying that living with two aspies has been both wonderful and awful. I worry that my daughter will get a strange idea about relationships but she loves her Dad, and she and I are very close. We discuss AS and what is normal, for lack of a better word, and what is not. I think she's got a pretty good handle on it. I think she is the best. There, honey, I did mention you.

*"Sharon", USA, 2000*

*30*

# O Negative

*Blood and guts don't bother me. When Rachel's finger was
    sliced open,*
*It was me, compressing it to stop the blood, saying this is
    going to need stitches.*
*It was me, pressing an ice pack on Julie's arm, knowing it
    was broken.*
*Hey, I'm the one happily watching the needle sink in, type O
    Negative.*

*There are so many other ways I'm certain I could be brave.*
*I could discover the body of a murder victim and not retch. I
    believe*
*I'd even lean in to get a closer look. I'd notice how the legs
    were splayed,*
*How blood has stuck in the hair, whether the eyes are open or
    closed.*

*I could be a nurse too. I'd bring the cool metal tools to the
    surgeon,*
*Sponge up the oozing blood. I'd inhale the rare sweetness of
    time*
*In the operating room, everything measured so precisely, so
    well-contained:*
*Beats of the heart, anesthetics, sponges, stitches, the miracle of
    oxygen.*

*I could even operate on you if I needed to. I could stick the
    scapel deep*
*Into your chest, pull back the skin, cut open the row of rib
    bones. I could reach*
*In and pull out your heart, I could do this and not faint. I
    could sew up any hole*
*Your heart may have, I'd work the needle and thread until it
    was as neat*
*As a queer needlepoint. I'm not bragging. This is just
    something I know.*

*I've always been cool and calm when fingers came
    unbuttoned.*
*But I must confess that if I held your thumping heart, I
    might feel something more,*
*Like I'd have to fight the urge to shake it, or maybe yell at it.
    I'd hold its baboom*
*baboom up to my ear, and then I might just put it back in
    your chest upside down.*

*I wish someone could tell me the right thing to do, or how I*
    *should feel.*
*When I think about my own heart's squirrel running so fast*
    *on its lonely treadmill,*
*I just want to sit down and cry. O I know I should stop*
    *being so negative.*
*Besides, I should be used to it, I'm a universal donor.*
    *Everyone wants my blood.*

*Anonymous, USA, 2002*

# 31

# Knowing is Understanding, Understanding is Accepting: A Note of Encouragement

We met one day at a conference in my country, where neither one of us lived at that time. He impressed me by his proficiency in my language, because, as a teacher, I know my language is difficult to learn. It was love at first sight. We saw each other as often as possible, which was not very often since we were separated by a sixteen-hour flight. We married exactly one year after the day we met.

Any marriage needs time to grow. Togetherness needs to grow. But trust and "we-feeling" never seemed to come. Understanding was non-existent. Communication rapidly ceased. Instead, we seemed to be competitors, and of course I needed to be the loser.

I gave up my career, I changed countries, my father passed on, but I could not leave the country to help comfort my mother. Those were very emotionally lonely days. And for everything, right down to the smallest details, I received the blame. Often I felt betrayed. I felt manipulated. I was expected to change, but in what? But I am not a quitter, so I stayed.

Our first child I felt was like me, right from birth. He happily looked around at everybody. He never cried. He was the perfect baby. However, his father did not know yet how to perform his father-role. He did not know how to take care of a baby or the mother. He thought he needed to establish his authority in the home by bullying everybody else. Finally, he escaped in his job: nights, days, anytime. It took me several years to get over the traumatic experiences that had surrounded my pregnancy and the birth of our first son.

Our second son was different from birth. Within the first twenty-four hours of his life his stomach was pumped three times, because they did not understand why he would not nurse. Reluctantly they let us go home. Eventually he would nurse, but after a while he would remember that he did not want to and he would cry out in frustration. Oh, he had so many frustrations: every feeding, every diaper change, every bath, every single little change was extremely unwelcome to this little one.

At fourteen months I concluded that his "terrible two" stage had already started. Every turn of the car caused major protest, because it was not what he had in mind. Eating and drinking would only happen when, what and where he decided. Changes of clothing caused more crying; we once took him to church with shoes taped to his feet. Whatever we did, or did not, after a little while he would remember it was all wrong and he would scream as if he was severely abused. It always drew attention and my only satisfaction was that friendly bystanders never could reason with him either. He would just continue to cry at full volume.

At age four he still had not outgrown his "terrible twos." He was not being atypical in growth, took all his milestones at the appropriate age. Yet I was at the verge of a nervous breakdown. My doctor prescribed Prozac, which helped tremendously in dealing with my husband, who was the opposite of support and blamed me for any signs of depression that I had started to show.

I decided to read up on autism, because his eye contact was very limited and social behavior basically absent. He would sit and page through books from the time he could sit up, so no wonder he could read by age four. He did not understand what he was reading though. His memory was amazing, but his interests were extremely limited. I wanted to have him tested and made the arrangements. The test results came back as "mild Asperger's Syndrome."

So I immediately started to read Tony Attwood's book on the subject. Then came the eye-openers, the *Aha-Erlebnis* as the Germans call it. The lights came on, the puzzle pieces fell in place. I was not only reading about my little son, who had only lived four years of his life. I was reading about my husband! There it was: no understanding for other people's emotions (yes, absolutely!), no feeling for social situations (so that's why I had to answer the questions his parents were asking him when we were visiting), scared of changes (and then to think I thought he was adventurous when I married him...), never apologetic, never ever taking any blame, unable to trust me, unable to listen and respond to me, the list went on and on.

This was good news for me! Knowing where certain behavior patterns originate helps me tremendously in taking emotional distance from the situation. I know now that he does not do it because he wants to hurt me. He does it because it is in his make-up to do it that way. Being a believer, I also found many answers to prayer (why God?) in the whole process of enlightenment that I went through. It also helped me to work on forgiveness for the many hurts of the past. The new understanding I found has helped me so much that I could wean myself from the Prozac. I think I can handle family life now that I understand so much more.

My husband accepted the diagnosis of our son in an easy manner. He read Tony Attwood's book. He knows we will have to invest much more effort in raising our son. Quite often he understands him better than I do and so he is more apt in coming up with solutions. Being more strict and extremely consequent in certain issues have produced sometimes dramatic improvements in our son's behavior. Now, at five years old, he has definitely outgrown the "terrible twos!" I am much more hopeful for his future.

I suspect my husband has learned more about himself too, but I doubt he will ever acknowledge he has Asperger. Instead he may suggest that I have it...

*Annemarieke, USA, 2002*

## 32

# The End into a Beginning

I must be crazy, my spouse says so.

I am a horrible parent, I am the scum of the earth.

I feel like a slave, no one appreciates the work I do for this family.

Do my feelings account for anything? Does anyone care that I hurt?

Death looks pretty attractive compared to this family life.

Everything is my fault, always. I am never right, it is just never enough.

How can a person who professed love, and some other vows, claim that I am irresponsible, immature, unreasonable, and unpleasant and still want to be married to me?

Why does my partner get to do certain things, but it is not acceptable for me to do the same?

Where did all my friends go?

Why don't we have friends over anymore, and more importantly, when did the invitations to our friends' houses cease?

Why does my spouse sleep so much, and why does it never seem to be enough.

Why do I not trust my spouse?

When did the communication break down to nonexistent? Why does my spouse not listen to me when I pour my heart out with emotion?

Boy, that was an odd thing my spouse did, hmmm, it must be me, I'm the crazy one.

My spouse forgot my birthday, our anniversary, told me that holidays are just another day, I don't like to celebrate, why should you?

My spouse inappropriately reprimands our children, sometimes physically, most of the time emotionally.

My spouse ignores the children's needs and wants and doesn't hear them a majority of the time.

When the children hurt themselves, my spouse always down plays the severity of the injury/illness – I have always been glad we saw the doctor unbeknownst to my spouse.

I rejoice when my spouse leaves the house and I can be myself.

I have insomnia, I am depressed, I have a panic disorder and a myriad of other physical ailments, all, I am sure, due from stress.

Why doesn't my spouse help me, I am doing 95% of all the work?

Why doesn't my spouse take care of things when I am sick, instead of claiming illness and sleeping all day?

Where are my compliments?

Why do I feel sabotaged when I am successful into feeling I am a failure?

Why do I get sucked into arguments I know will not end in a win/win situation, or with any compromising?

How can we have a nasty fight and then 10 minutes later my spouse is acting like nothing is wrong after nothing was settled?

Why does my spouse start eating before I sit down to the table, and is done before I pick up my fork?

Why can't my spouse find personal items?

Why isn't my spouse more organized?

Why do the simplest tasks seem so difficult for my spouse?

Why do I feel like my spouse is an extra child and I am the Mother?

How can I control my spouse's spending?

How many more electronics and tools can we possibly fit into this house?

Of course the electronics get used, the tools do not.

If something breaks, why is it my fault?

Why is blame so important to my spouse?

If we need to fix some major household item, why must I threaten to call a professional before it gets fixed?

Why does my spouse fix things that are not broken, so that then, they become broken?

Will my spouse ever choose different clothes to wear?

Will the verbal abuse ever end?"

These are just a few of the questions and statements that have been running through my mind. Does this sound like you? If it does there may be a very good reason for your thoughts like these. There are many, many more, believe me, because I know. There are reasons for your feelings, there always are, and they need to be validated. So, don't ignore them. Listen to them, follow their direction. Be true to yourself. You cannot change your spouse, but you can change you and how you cope, handle and deal with everyday life. Make this the End into the Beginning. Join us in spreading the knowledge, come find a home amongst those who understand your fears, heart ache, depression and frustrations. We do know, because we all live it every day, of every week, of every month, of every year. Welcome Home!

*Anonymous, USA, 1999*

**The Beginning**

"The Beginning" is dedicated by the author to: my children, Dr Tony Attwood, Karen Rodman, Brenda Wall, and all those who accompany me daily on my journey.

"The End into a Beginning" was written four years ago by a woman I hardly see or recognize any longer. A woman who has groaned, grunted, grieved and grown in so many different, positive and connected ways. Little did I know four years ago how true the words "The End into a Beginning" would become for me. This is my journey. My hope and prayer is that what I have learned will be of use and can help you in your own personal journey. The *groar* we roar must be "One Voice" that is unified, loud and frequent. Little *groars* always turn into BIG ones; never underestimate the power of any *groar.*

Where to begin? At the "beginning" of course! I have known my undiagnosed Asperger's Syndrome husband for thirty-five years, we have been married for nineteen years. Before entering into therapy on my own, I was at the brink of a nervous breakdown. My body was betraying me physically, I never felt well, every part of me hurt all of the time. Sleep, what was that? And how I longed for a long, deep and restful sleep. My health had been severly compromised for many years. I am healthier now than I have ever been. How can this be, you ask?

I started with very small, baby steps. With the help of my counselor, Dr Tony Attwood, my family at the FAAAS Inc. list, and some well-written self-help books by Dr Phillip McGraw, Don Miguel Ruiz and many others, I began to redefine myself. The self I knew was still in me, somewhere down deep, the young woman who had hopes, dreams and aspirations. The self I knew that was lost, and not totally for reasons of her own doing. Every day I would wake up and ask myself, "Just for today, what absolutely needs to be done, what one thing is bothering me and, the most important, where is my down/rest time for today?" I would list the minimum "had to do today" items. I would pick the one "thing" that was bugging me and either make restitution with the situation by letting it go, giving it to God/Universe, or do something about it – remember, one thing at a time, only one thing. And I would schedule down or rest time for myself – I never faltered on this, never. If it meant unplugging the phone, drawing the drapes shut, whatever it took to get my time, I did it.

As days, weeks, months and now years have passed, I became the person I have wanted to be! Although the price was, at times, very high for my family around me, it was worth every step I took. I strive to always be respectful, compassionate and caring of others, but without compromising myself in the process. It is okay to have different views, opinions, and ways of doing things. I celebrate diversity at every chance that presents itself to me. I smile at everyone I make eye contact with – you would be surprised at some of the reactions I get!

Currently, my family is going through a divorce. I have been preparing for four years for this event. Although I did not anticipate going through divorce so soon, I was glad that I had been as prepared as I could have. Again, very small steps. The most important, ever-changing and time-consuming step was keeping the "leaving plan" in order, current and attainable in a moment's notice. Not an easy task when children are involved, not impossible either. This plan will look different for each individual but should include basics: a safe place for yourself/children /pets that can be accessed immediately if necessary; a stash of cash to last at least two months if possible; always keep half a tank of gas in your vehicle, no excuses; a resource for food storage and stock the pantry (make sure you rotate the stock occasionally); make arrangements (if possible) for pre-scription medications; any other item that is unique to your situation that can be secured before the disaster – think proactive. Some things to think about: obtain a credit card in your name solely; have your own personal checking/savings accounts; if you are leaving the residence, remove your name from all bills, utilities, credit cards, etc., that you can without being detected. Make an appointment with a lawyer and just talk for one hour (believe me, if you are prepared this is more than enough!) about your rights and what you can expect should you choose to or need to file for divorce. If you like this lawyer, educate him or her now about AS – it will be an asset in your future. Do not, I repeat, *do not* wait until you are in a divorce to educate this person – you will live to regret it. Remember, AS spouses most likely are adept at acting, manipulation and getting things their way. This is not the time for that scenario; this will be the time to set your boundaries and stick by them with the law behind you. Educate your lawyer and his or her staff even if they do not realize they are being educated, and remember you are paying them. They can be fired by you.

One final important step that must be taken. You must document every incident and conversation through your own journalizing (very healing by the way!), with pediatricians, therapists, doctors, lawyers, community services, anyone who is helping your family, has a file/chart on any member of your family (with exception of the AS adult) or you think can and will help when you need to call on them. Make your own copies to leave with them and ask the professional "Would you keep this in our records please?" Guess what happens? You are obviously documenting everything, but the professional is bound to read what you have submitted; you've got a *groar* going – educate, educate, educate. I cannot stress enough how important it is to keep good relationships with the people who will be your team.

Good communication with these folks will be returned to you a thousand fold.

That's "The Beginning" as of today. Our life is better without my AS husband; however, there are other challenges that have arisen from my decision. For me, I find that decisions are made more quickly, every issue is dealt with and we move on to the next, the children and I are exploring things that we were kept away from and for the first time we are happy, laughing (even having fun) and enjoying each other.

This too can be your life, if you set it up that way! Good luck and may God or the Universe Bless and Keep You and Yours.

*Anonymous, USA, 2002*

## 33

# Untitled

As well as having lived in a marriage to a man who was diagnosed with Asperger's Syndrome, I work as a counselor and have published two books on the subject of couple relationships affected by Asperger's Syndrome.

Through my research I have met many couples and through my work have counseled many more. My time has been dedicated to gaining information and increasing awareness of the effect that Asperger's Syndrome can have on a couple relationship.

Relationships where one or both partners are affected by Asperger's Syndrome are not all negative and destructive; there are those that have many positive points and have survived the rigours of time. Most of these are the relationships where Asperger's Syndrome is known and accepted by both partners. The couple can then develop an awareness of what effect Asperger's Syndrome can have on a relationship and, if both are willing, can work together at increasing their understanding of the syndrome.

Unfortunately, the possibility that Asperger's Syndrome is responsible for many of the problems is not always known or accepted. This may be because of lack of awareness, misdiagnosis or a complete denial by the partner who has the syndrome. Any of these reasons can result in the neurotypical (NT) partner being blamed for all the problems the relationship is facing. Until the public and professionals achieve full awareness of Asperger's Syndrome and support and guidance is available to the couple, both partners in the relationship will continue to suffer. Couples sometimes struggle for years to keep together a dysfunctional relationship with no knowledge of why their attempts keep crashing down.

Awareness can especially help the NT partner find ways to compensate for the lack of empathy and emotional support that he or she often will have been silently suffering for years.

The voice of FAAAS has gained in power and offers valuable support for many NT partners who have come to realize that they are in a relationship with one who has Asperger's Syndrome. FAAAS is about awareness and with awareness comes understanding. Only through understanding Asperger's Syndrome, and how it will affect the relationship, will the NT partner be able to make an informed choice on whether he or she feels the relationship can survive. This is when the vital support and advice from groups such as FAAAS can be crucial. Long live FAAAS!

*Maxine Aston, author of* **The Other Half of Asperger Syndrome**, *UK, 2002*

# 34

# Come With Me

Hold my hand and come with me
I'll show you what life was meant to be
Filled with love, joy and empathy
To be shared with family, friends and especially me

A Child forever you will be
Suffering in silence engulfed with misery
Prejudice is not your way
Sadly you fall victim, become its prey

It breaks my heart to have to see
Autism has taken you from me
In its arms you struggle to be free
If only I could find the key

I search; I look and yell out loud
This puzzle it remains yet a mystery
I hold on to the dream you see
That one day you'll be back with me

Turmoil and confusion for the world to see
A connection I need, it has to be
Pain, sadness forever etched within me
An eternity I shall wait if that is how it should be

In the meantime I struggle to construe
Routines and rigidity from inflexible you

Autism, Asperger or PDD
Wake Up! Everyone
Take a look you'll see
Captured is the very essence of society

My husband and my precious son
I reach out my hand for you to come
Hold on tight and follow me
I want to show you what life was meant to be

*Dawn O'Neil, USA, 2002*

# Afterword

## Developing relationships

Men and women with Asperger's Syndrome can develop intimate personal relationships and each can become a life-long partner and parent. For such a relationship to begin, both parties would initially have found the other person to be attractive. What are the characteristics that women find attractive in men with Asperger's Syndrome? From my clinical experience and the research of Maxine Aston (2003) there are numerous positive attributes. Many women describe their first impression of their husband as being someone who is kind, attentive and caring. Another positive attribute can be that of the "handsome and silent stranger". The person with Asperger's Syndrome may have symmetrical facial features that are aesthetically appealing. He may be more handsome than previous boyfriends and considered a good "catch" in terms of looks, especially if the partner has doubts regarding her own physical attractiveness. The lack of social and conversational skills can be attributed to the "silent stranger" whose social abilities will be unlocked and transformed by a partner who is an expert in empathy and socializing. There can be a maternal compassion for the man's limited social abilities, with a belief that his social confusion and lack of social confidence is due to aspects of his childhood, and can be repaired over time.

The attractiveness of the man with Asperger's Syndrome is enhanced by his intellectual abilities, career prospects, creativity and degree of attention to his partner. This devotion to his partner can be very flattering, although others could perceive the adulation as bordering on being obsessive. His hobby or special interest can initially be perceived as endearing and "typical of boys and men". The first meeting may be through a shared interest, such as music, theatre, the care of animals or similar religious or political beliefs (Aston 2003). The person may be admired for speaking his mind, having a strong sense of social justice and being a man of principle. He can be described as a "gentleman", with old world values, not as motivated towards physically intimate activities.

When asked, "What was initially attractive in your partner?", men with Asperger's Syndrome have often described some physical quality, such as hair or eyes, or personality characteristics such as being maternal or having nurturing qualities. They may be less attentive to physical proportions than are other men, and also not concerned about age or cultural differences. They may actively choose someone with demonstrable social and maternal abilities and at the opposite end of the empathy continuum. They know they need a partner who is a guide in social situations. They may also know they need a partner who can act as an executive secretary to help with organizational problems.

The courtship may not be an indication of the problems that can develop later in the relationship. The man with Asperger's Syndrome may have developed a superficial expertise in romance and dating from careful observation and mimicking of television programs and films. His partner can be enthralled by his attentiveness and adulation. He is less likely to want to be with his male friends or seek other relationships. His persistence to formalize the relationship may be hard to resist. The person with Asperger's Syndrome may also seek someone who has strong moral values, who, once married, is likely to be dedicated to making the relationship succeed.

**Subsequent experiences**
The person who does not have Asperger's Syndrome may be in love with his or her partner, but is the nature and expression of love reciprocal? Research has identified a characteristic of Asperger's Syndrome called "impaired Theory of Mind", namely difficulties with the conceptualisation of feelings and desires of others and oneself. Mayes, Cohen and Klin (1993) have examined desire and fantasy from a psychoanalytic perspective in the context of impaired Theory of Mind in people with Asperger's Syndrome. Their view is that people with Asperger's Syndrome do not fall in love readily, nor grieve the loss of others to the degree one would expect. Their description is that "generally, their responses to losses are as muted and brief as their displays of affection" (p.460). In his autobiography, Edgar Schneider (1999) explains his confusion regarding love and grief:

> At one point my mother, exasperated at me, said, "You know what the trouble is? You don't know how to love!

You need to learn how to love!" I was taken aback totally. I hadn't the faintest notion what she meant. I still don't. (p.43)

The author has conducted relationship counseling for couples where one partner has a diagnosis of Asperger's Syndrome. Each partner is asked to give his or her description of love. The following are the thoughts of several partners who do not share their husband's diagnosis of Asperger's Syndrome:

Love is: Tolerance, non-judgemental, supportive.

Love is: A complex of beliefs that tap into our child-hood languages and experiences; it is inspired when you meet someone that has a quality that maybe you admire, or do not have (admiration and respect) – or that they (someone you admire) reflect back to your ideal self – which is what you want to be or see yourself as.

Love is: Passion, acceptance, affection, reassurance, mutual enjoyment.

Love is: What I feel for myself when I am with another person.

The following are some of the descriptions given by their husbands with Asperger's Syndrome:

Love is: Helping and doing things for your lover.

Love is: An attempt to connect to the other person's feelings and emotions.

Love is: Companionship, someone to depend on to help you in the right direction.

Love is: I have no idea what is involved.

Love is: Tolerance, loyal, allows "space".

The person with Asperger's Syndrome may express his or her love in more practical terms; or, to change a quote from Star Trek (as Spock is examining an extra-terrestrial): "It's life, Jim, but not as we know it". In Asperger's Syndrome, it is love, but not as we know it.

After the "honeymoon" period, there can be a gradual realization of the nature of the relationship, and disappointment and stress for both partners. The non-Asperger's Syndrome partner can begin to feel rejected and lonely. Moments of physical contact and affection can be described as "hugging a piece of wood". Times of distress, when empathy and words and gestures of love would be expected, may simply result in being left alone to "get over it". The author has noted that this is not a callous act. The most effective emotional restorative for people with Asperger's Syndrome is solitude. They often describe how a hug is perceived as "an uncomfortable squeeze" and does not automatically make them feel better. Being alone is their main recovery mechanism and they may assume that is also the case for their partner. They may also not know how to respond, or fear making the situation worse. The author observed a situation where a husband with Asperger's Syndrome was sitting next to his wife who was in tears. He remained still and did not offer any words or gestures of affection. Later, when discussing this situation he was asked if he noticed that his wife was crying; he replied, "Yes, but I didn't want to do the wrong thing".

The optimism of the partner who does not have Asperger's Syndrome that his or her partner will gradually change and become socially skilled and confident, can dissolve into despair that social skills are static due to limited motivation to be more sociable. This can be due to the intellectual effort needed to socialize, subsequent exhaustion, and fear of making a social mistake. Joint social contact with friends can slowly diminish. The partner with Asperger's Syndrome does not want or need the same degree of social contact as he or she had when courting. The non-Asperger's Syndrome partner may reluctantly agree to reduce the frequency and duration of social contact with family, friends and colleagues for the sake of the relationship. The partner gradually absorbs the characteristics of Asperger's Syndrome into their own personality.

In any relationship, there will inevitably be areas of disagreement and conflict. Unfortunately, people with Asperger's Syndrome can have a history of limited ability to successfully manage conflict. They may have a limited range of options and may not be skilled in the art of negotiation, accepting alternative perspectives and agreeing to compromise. There can be an inability to accept even partial responsibility. Partners complain "It is never his fault" and " I always get the blame". There can be concerns about verbal abuse, especially as a response to perceived criticism, with an apparent inability to show remorse and to forgive and forget. This can be due to a difficulty with understanding the thoughts, feelings and perspectives of others, a central characteristic of Asperger's Syndrome.

There can be problems with what psychologists call "executive function": that is, planning, organizational skills, time management and flexibility in thinking. Life can become regimented. There has been a suggestion that

Napoleon had signs of Asperger's Syndrome; the non-Asperger's Syndrome partner can feel he or she is not an equal but has to take orders from "the general" who meticulously prepares and considers every detail of the logistics. The partner with Asperger's Syndrome can impose his or her decisions, an approach the author calls the "Frank Sinatra syndrome": "I did it my way". This regimented approach can be an attempt to overcome problems with executive function. At the other extreme, the person may be so incompetent with executive functioning that his or her partner has to take the responsibility for budgeting, planning and career guidance. This adds to the inequality in the relationship.

There can also be a lack of an understanding of the importance of romance and physical intimacy in the relationship. During a counseling session, the wife of a man with Asperger's Syndrome explained her distress that they had not had sex for over a year. Her husband's reply was to ask her why she would want sex when they had enough children. There can be conflict regarding the differing levels of desire, the frequency and value of intimacy.

People with Asperger's Syndrome are prone to having difficulties with emotion management. We are not sure if this is a constitutional feature of Asperger's Syndrome or a reaction to the stress of coping with the social and changing aspects of family life and work. The person may develop signs of cyclical depression, anxiety disorders or episodes of intense anger. His or her partner may try to use affection and talking about feelings to improve the partner's mood but these strategies may not be successful for people with Asperger's Syndrome. They can be less able to communicate their feelings in speech and conversation, whether they are positive emotions such as love and happiness or negative emotions such as sadness and worry. Feelings of frustration and anger can be expressed in brief, dramatic and destructive actions. This can lead to a feeling of tension in the household and avoidance of antagonising the person with Asperger's Syndrome.

When children come in the relationship, the partner with Asperger's Syndrome becomes a parent but may not have the intuitive understanding of how to be a father or mother. His or her partner may notice that he or she also rarely provides emotional support to the children. There can be conflicts in terms of management strategies, and sharing of chores and responsibilities, and in tolerance of the normal behaviors of childhood and adolescence. Those who do not have Asperger's Syndrome can also notice their partner's emotional immaturity and rivalry with the children, and feel they have become a solo parent; they may long for the partner they expected and need.

People with Asperger's Syndrome can also be disappointed in how the relationship has developed. They can recognize the changing expectations and feel great stress, as they are unsure what to do as a long-term partner and parent. Their partner expects them to know intuitively what to do but that intuition may not be there. The enjoyable and relatively simple courtship is replaced with changing responsibilities. They can be unsure of what to do and escape into their work, hobby or special interest. Women with Asperger's Syndrome can recognize that their husband and society expect them to easily express love for their partner and children, and they realize that this typical female role is not a natural part of their character.

## The importance and acceptance of a diagnosis

Understanding the nature of Asperger's Syndrome can be crucial for the individual and the relationship. The acceptance of the diagnosis can enable the adult with Asperger's Syndrome to be aware of his or her abilities and difficulties, and acknowledge the work that needs to be done to improve the quality of the relationships within the family and between the partners. The chapter by Maxine Aston clearly establishes that one of the keys to a successful relationship is acceptance of the diagnosis by both parties.

The first step to improving the relationship is to obtain a diagnosis. This can be a problem as there are few specialists with sufficient experience in the diagnosis and treatment of adults with Asperger's Syndrome. There can be reluctance by the partner who may have Asperger's Syndrome to arrange a diagnostic appointment with a clinical psychologist or psychiatrist, because of the fear of being diagnosed as having a psychiatric illness and being labelled as "mad". Another problem is that the diagnostic criteria are primarily designed to identify signs in children. We have yet to establish consistent diagnostic assessment procedures for adults. A visit to an inexperienced clinician can result in a rejection of the diagnosis, as he or she may be less aware of how successful some adults with Asperger's Syndrome can be in camouflaging their problems and providing answers that appear to imply social competence. The diagnostic assessment requires careful consideration of information from the individual, but also independent and objective information on his or her childhood and current relationship from the partner.

Once the diagnosis has been confirmed, there is no guarantee that the person with Asperger's Syndrome accepts it. To accept the diagnosis, the person must then undertake a major re-examination of him- or herself and acknowledge that previous compensatory mechanisms and automatic behaviors will have to be changed. This is no easy task and the first reaction can be to deny the diagnosis. Given time and further explanations of the nature of Asperger's Syndrome and the positive changes that can be achieved in the relationship and within the family due to acceptance of the diagnosis, there can be an eventual acceptance, and potential for improvement in the relationship. If there is no acceptance then the opportunities for a more successful relationship can be impaired significantly. In contrast, some partners are greatly relieved to finally have an explanation of why they are different. They may have known they were different from early childhood and developed low self-esteem, or an arrogant denial that they had any problems with social reasoning and empathy. At last there is an explanation and an understanding that has been elusive all their life.

The next stage is to explain the nature of Asperger's Syndrome to the children, extended family, friends and relationship counselors. The children will have recognized that the parent with Asperger's Syndrome is unusual, especially if they have had opportunities to stay overnight, or go on vacation, with friends. They can feel that their father or mother with Asperger's Syndrome does not really understand them, is more likely to criticize than make a compliment, and may not be fun to play with.

Indeed, parents with Asperger's Syndrome may not know how to play with their children or show acceptance and affection. They can be intolerant of any noise or interruption and actively oppose any of their children's friends visiting their home. They may put intense pressure on their children to achieve academic success, such that the children think they are not loved for who they are but what they achieve. The children may also be fearful of their parent's mood when frustrated or angry, or of the "cold" touch of rare affection.

In adolescence, there can also be confusion as to why the non-Asperger's Syndrome parent tolerates the relationship. The children may feel rejected, and may respond to living in such a household by striving to seek approval, escaping to stay with other families and leaving home as soon as possible to create an alternative and more typical home. When children understand the way Asperger's Syndrome has affected their mother or father there can be a realization that their parent has a genuine difficulty understanding and expressing affection, which is not due to any fault in themselves, and that their parent's unusual behavior is a form of compensation for having Asperger's Syndrome.

## Strategies to improve the relationship

Once the diagnosis is understood and accepted, there are strategies that can improve the relationships between the two partners, and the parent with Asperger's Syndrome and his or her children. The author has identified several pre-requisites for a successful relationship. The first is mutual acceptance of the diagnosis. The second is motivation to change. One of the characteristics of Asperger's Syndrome is the desire to become an expert and to thoroughly explore a topic. When the partner is motivated to learn how to improve the relationship, all he or she needs is access to information, time and guidance.

Some of the information is now available as literature (Aston 2001, Aston 2003; Slater-Walker and Slater-Walker 2002; Stanford 2003). However, it may be extremely valuable to have support and guidance from a relationship counselor who has knowledge and experience of couples where one partner has Asperger's Syndrome. There are currently plans to increase the training of relationship counselors to improve their ability to identify signs of Asperger's Syndrome and modify conventional counseling to accommodate the unusual profile of abilities.

We now have several web based support groups such as www.faaas.org and www.justgathertogether.com/aspires.html that can provide forums for empathy and advice from fellow partners. Several psychologists, such as the author, are specialising in relationship and sexuality therapy exclusively designed for adults with Asperger's Syndrome. The support group FAAAS has also convened weekend workshops for partners that have been facilitated by specialists in Asperger's Syndrome. The papers, transcripts, audio and video recordings of these annual workshops are available from the website www.faaas.org.

Other strategies to help improve the relationships can include the development by the non-Asperger's Syndrome partner of an independent social life to satisfy his or her need for greater social experiences; programs to encourage the expression of affection and sexuality; improvements in communication and decision-making; and the sharing of responsibilities.

The improvement in communication can take unusual forms, for example, the thoughts and feelings of the person with Asperger's Syndrome may be more accurately and eloquently expressed in an email to his or her partner. Since childhood, the person with Asperger's Syndrome has had, by definition, difficulties with non-verbal behaviors, social and emotional reciprocity and understanding the thoughts and feelings of others. He or she will need guidance and encouragement in becoming an equal in the relationship. We now have programs, initially developed for children, but now applicable to adults, to teach emotion recognition, empathy and the pragmatic aspects of language. One example is the new program, "Mind Reading: the interactive guide to emotions", developed at the University of Cambridge. Further information on this program is available at www.human-emotions.com. We also hope that as young children are diagnosed, early and continuing intervention to increase social reasoning, emotional maturity and management, empathy, friendship and relationship skills, and organizational skills will prevent or reduce some of the problems that can occur for adults with Asperger's Syndrome.

Finally, we are starting to develop programs to help parents with Asperger's Syndrome improve their understanding of their children and to improve their abilities as a parent. Perhaps the first advice is for them to recognize the natural parenting abilities of their non-Asperger's Syndrome partners; if in doubt, they should seek and accept the advice of their partner. Another approach is to read the numerous books on child rearing and stages of child development. These practical reference guides can be of considerable assistance in improving knowledge and abilities in being a successful parent. Thus, although there can be considerable despair when one examines the relationships of men and women with Asperger's Syndrome, there is hope in terms of our new understanding and the practical strategies which exist to improve the ability to be a successful and loved partner and parent.

*Dr Tony Attwood*

## References

Aston, M. (2001) *The Other Half of Asperger Syndrome: A guide to living in an intimate relationship with a partner who has Asperger Syndrome.* London: The National Autistic Society.

Aston, M. (2003) *Aspergers in Love: Couple relationships and family affairs.* London: Jessica Kingsley Publishers.

Mayes, L., Cohen, D. and Klin, A. (1993) "Desire and fantasy: a psychoanalytic perspective on theory of mind and autism." In S. Baron-Cohen, T. Tager-Flusberg and D. Cohen (eds) *Understanding Other Minds: Perspectives from Autism.* Oxford: Oxford Medical Publications.

Schneider, E. (1999) *Discovering My Autism.* London: Jessica Kingsley Publishers.

Slater-Walker, G. and Slater-Walker, C. (2002) *An Asperger Marriage.* London: Jessica Kingsley Publishers.

Stanford, A. (2003) *Asperger Syndrome and Long-Term Relationships.* London: Jessica Kingsley Publishers.

13881385R00106

Made in the USA
Lexington, KY
25 February 2012